Auntie V.'s

Faces of

Dia de los Muertos

An Adult Coloring Book

By: V. PEREIRA

Auntie V.'s Faces of Dia de los Muertos

By: Auntie Vs' Coloring Books For Adults

© 2015 V. Pereira

ISBN-13: 978-1522735137

ISBN-10: 1522735135

DEDICATION

To all my sweet Grand Babies:

Marisa, Stevie, Carlitos,

Alivia, Isaiah, Samuel and Angel.....

.....Especially to Baby James Angelo.

And lastly, to the child within us all...

And to Toya and Son -Thanks for your

support and for believing in me!

Visit us online:

FACEBOOK: https://www.facebook.com/auntievscoloringbooksforadults/

TWITTER: https://twitter.com/AuntieVs

BLOG: https://auntievs.wordpress.com/

AUTHOR CENTRAL: https://www.amazon.com/author/auntiev

Look for Auntie V.'s other coloring books on Amazon:

Adult Coloring Book Valentine's Day

http://www.amazon.com/dp/1523366737

Día de los Muertos or Day of the Dead is a three day celebration of the dead with October 31st,

being the day of **Angelitos** or spirits of children.

November 1st is **All Saints Day** for Adult Spirits and November 2nd is **All Souls Day**. The day which

families visit the graves of their dead.

Families sometimes build alters, at home or the cemetery, where they place **'offerendas'.**

Among other things, these 'offerendas' can be favorite items and foods of the departed such as

fruits and nuts, cigarettes or **pan de muerto**, a special sweet bread called 'pan de muerto' or in

the United States, 'bread of dead', which is prepared in the weeks before the Dias de Muertos celebrations.

The people decorate with **papel picado**, **sugar skulls** and **cardboard skeletons** as well as painting

caliveras (or skulls) on their faces.

Celebrations can sometimes become humorous as

people remember the antics and funny ways of their departed.

Some see painting **Calaveras** or skulls on your face as a way to get in touch with the darker side of

ones self and to come to terms with death.

We hope you enjoy coloring The Faces of the Dia de los Muertos!

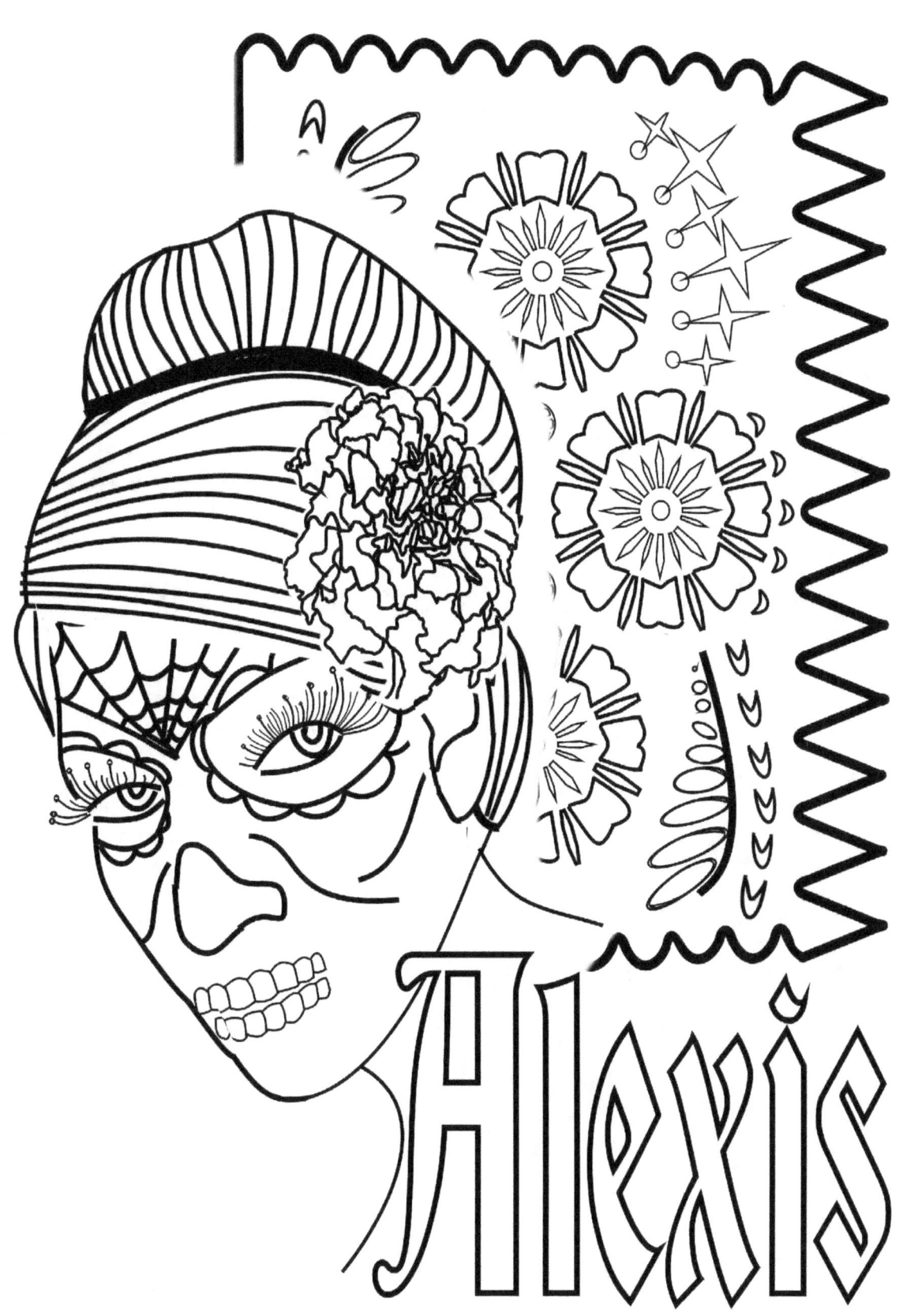

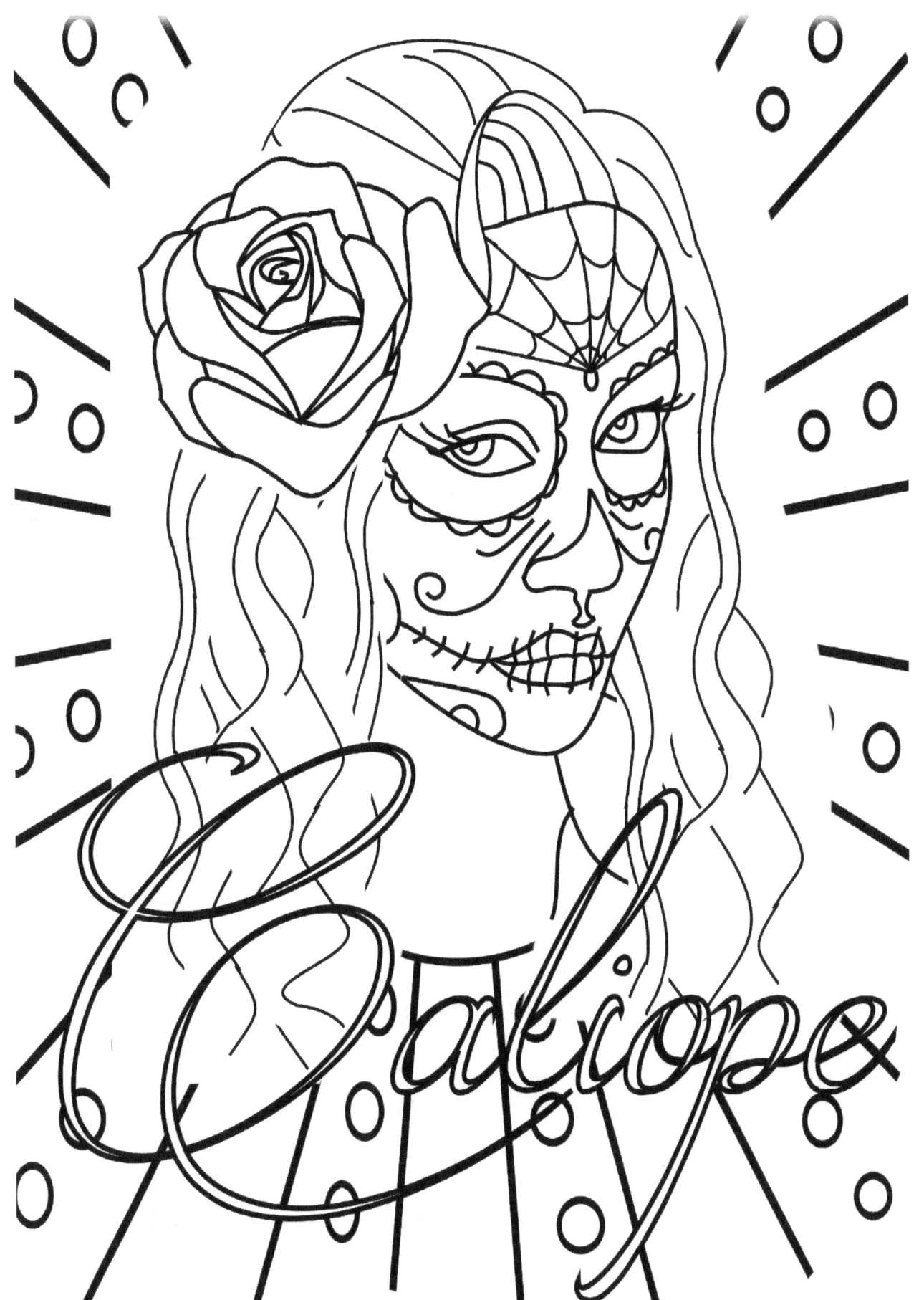

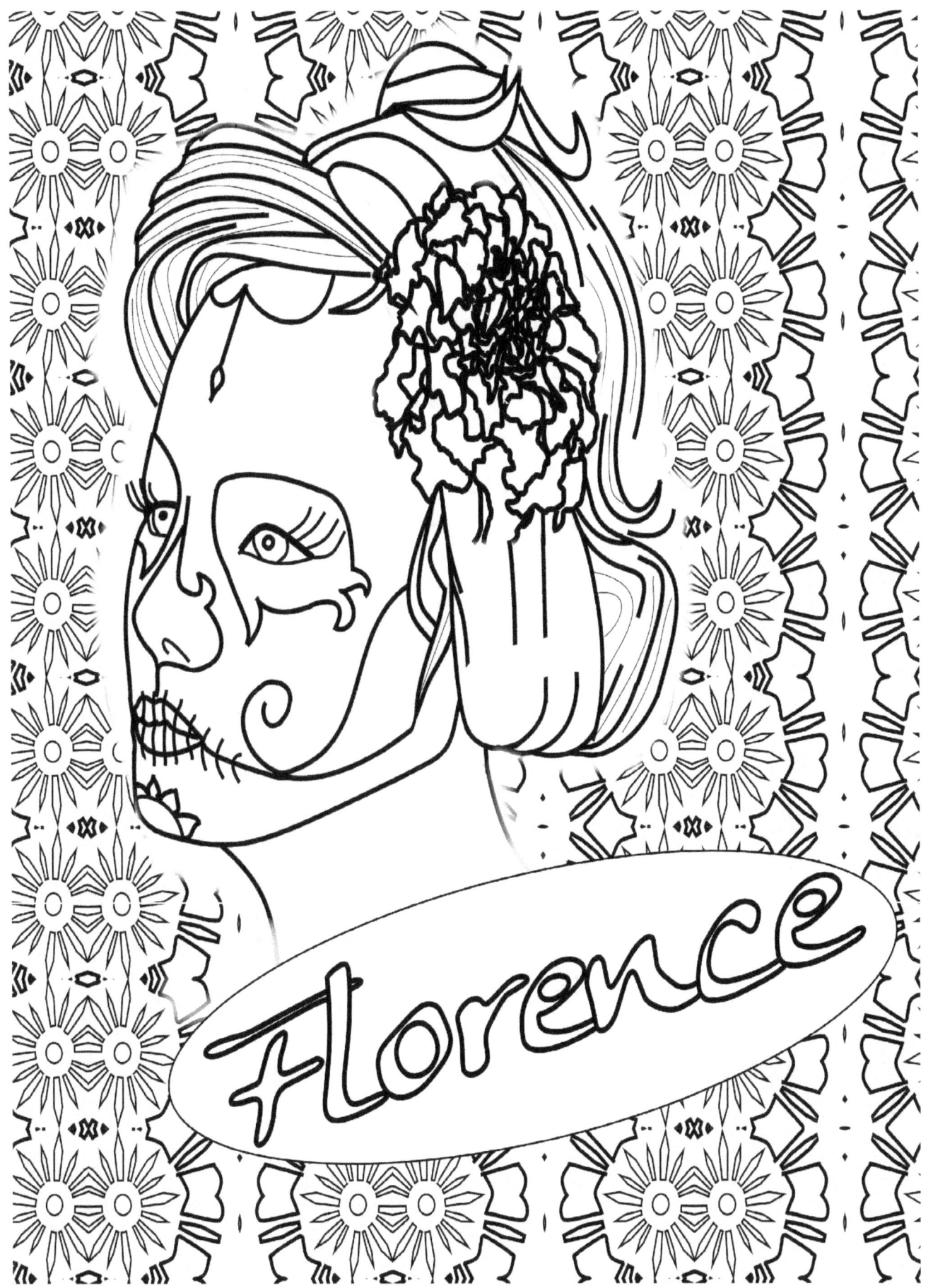

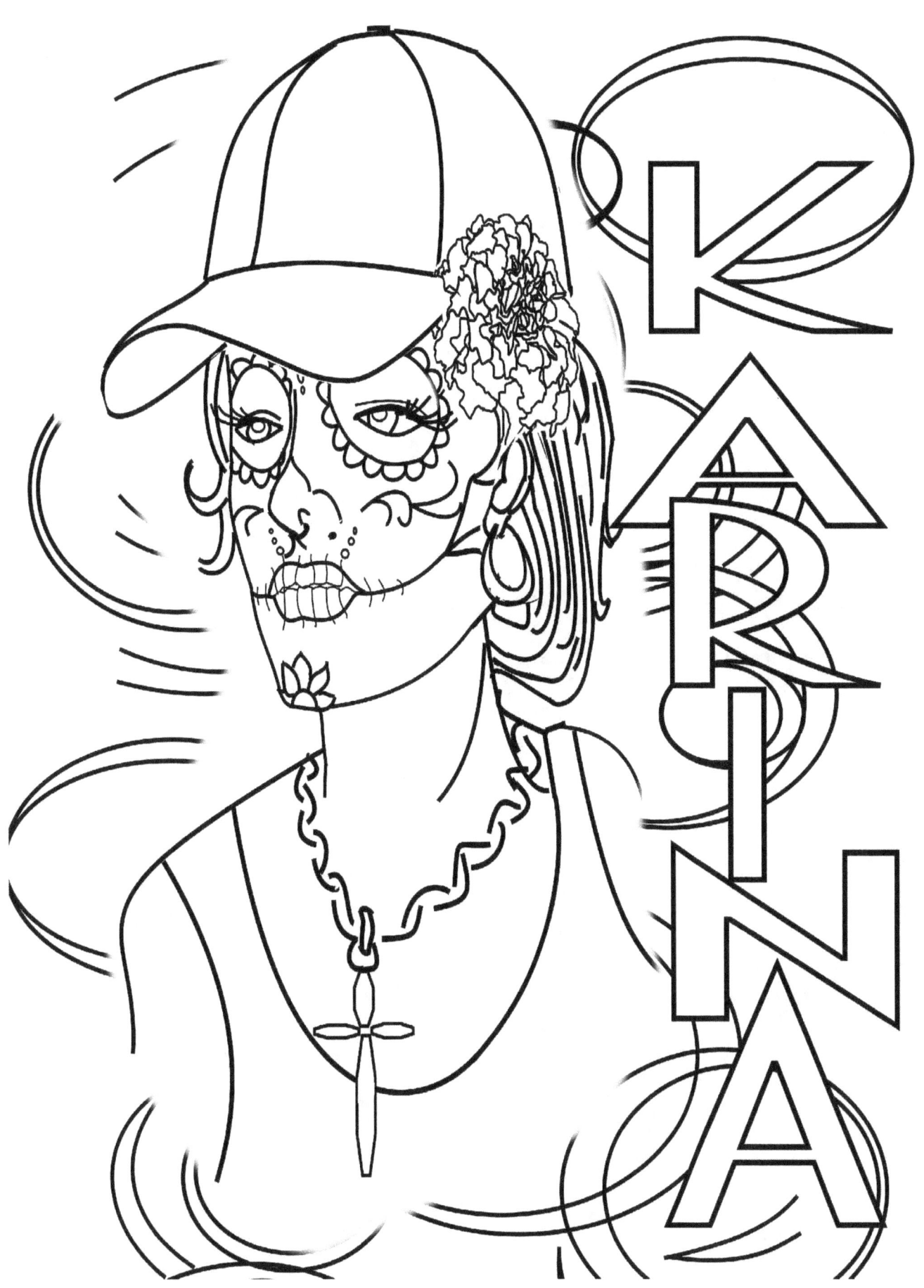

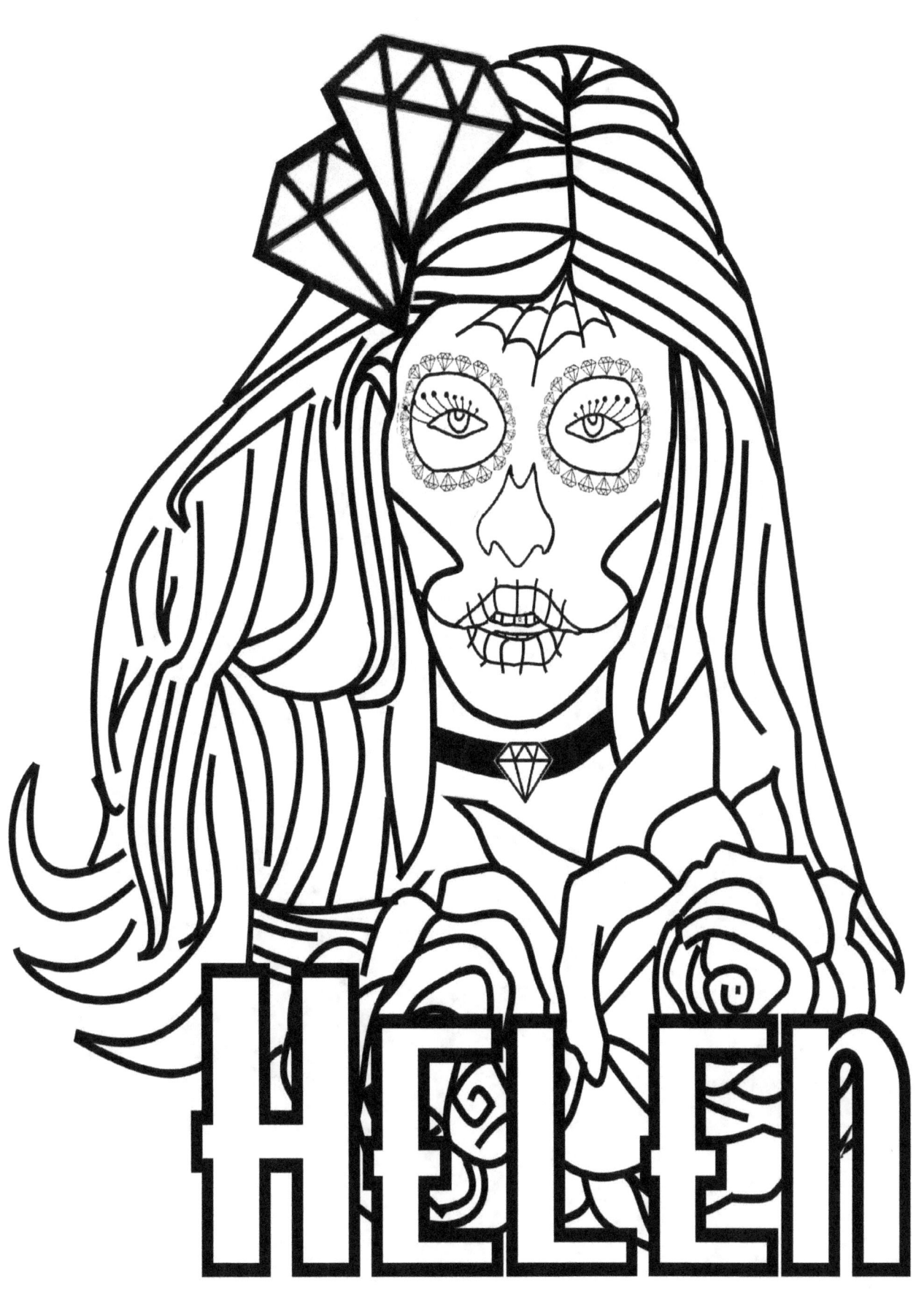

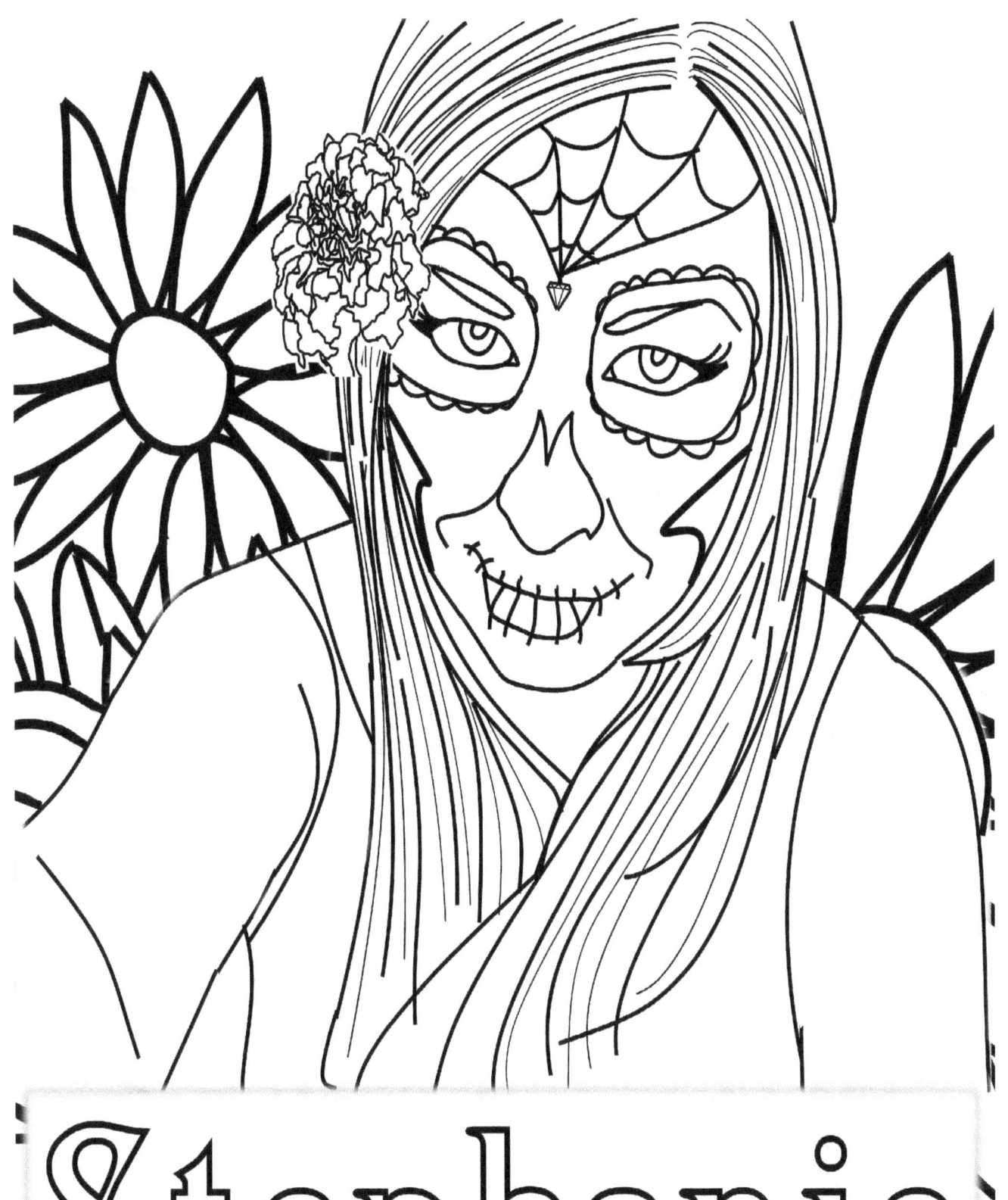

Stephanie

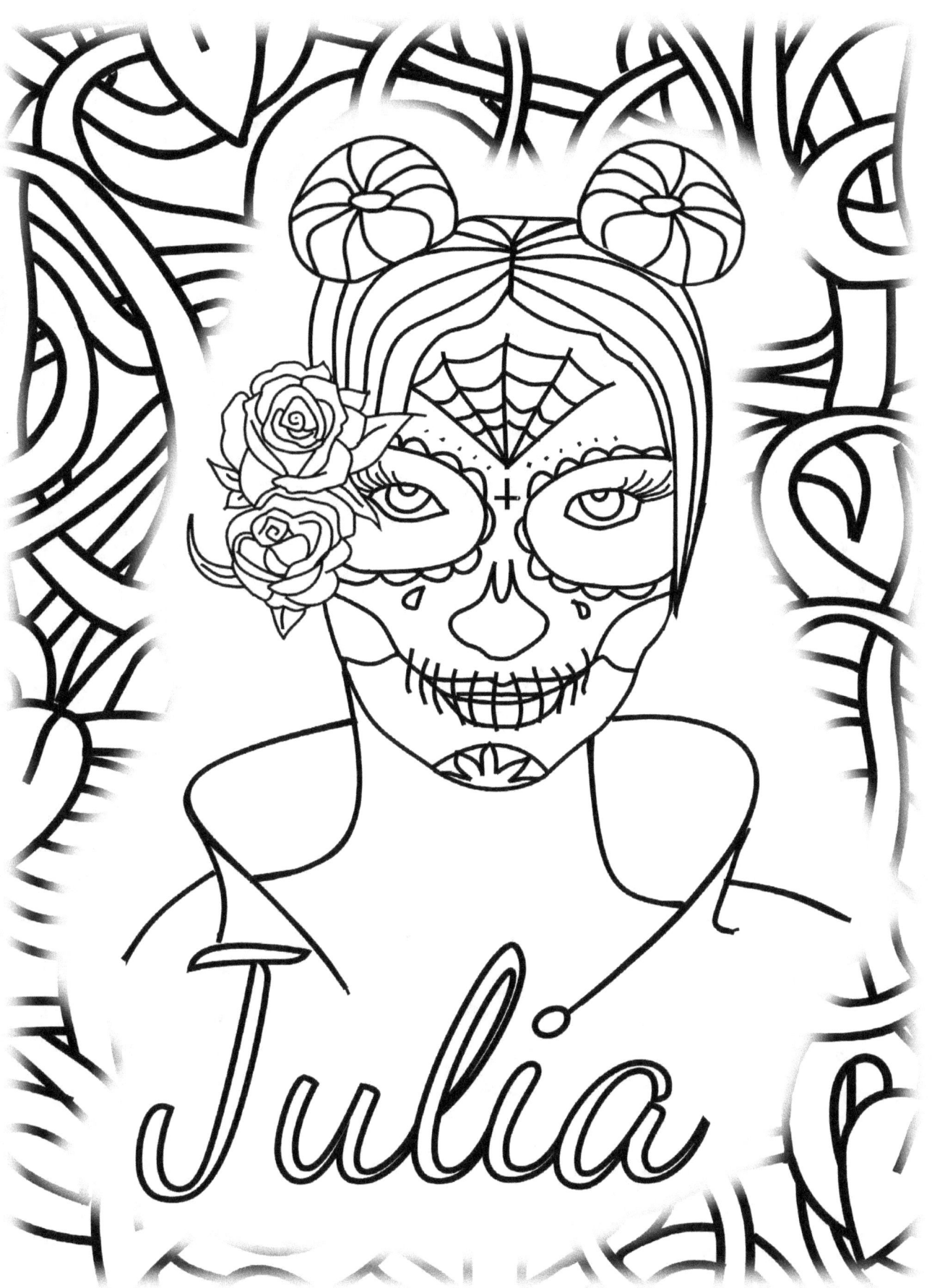

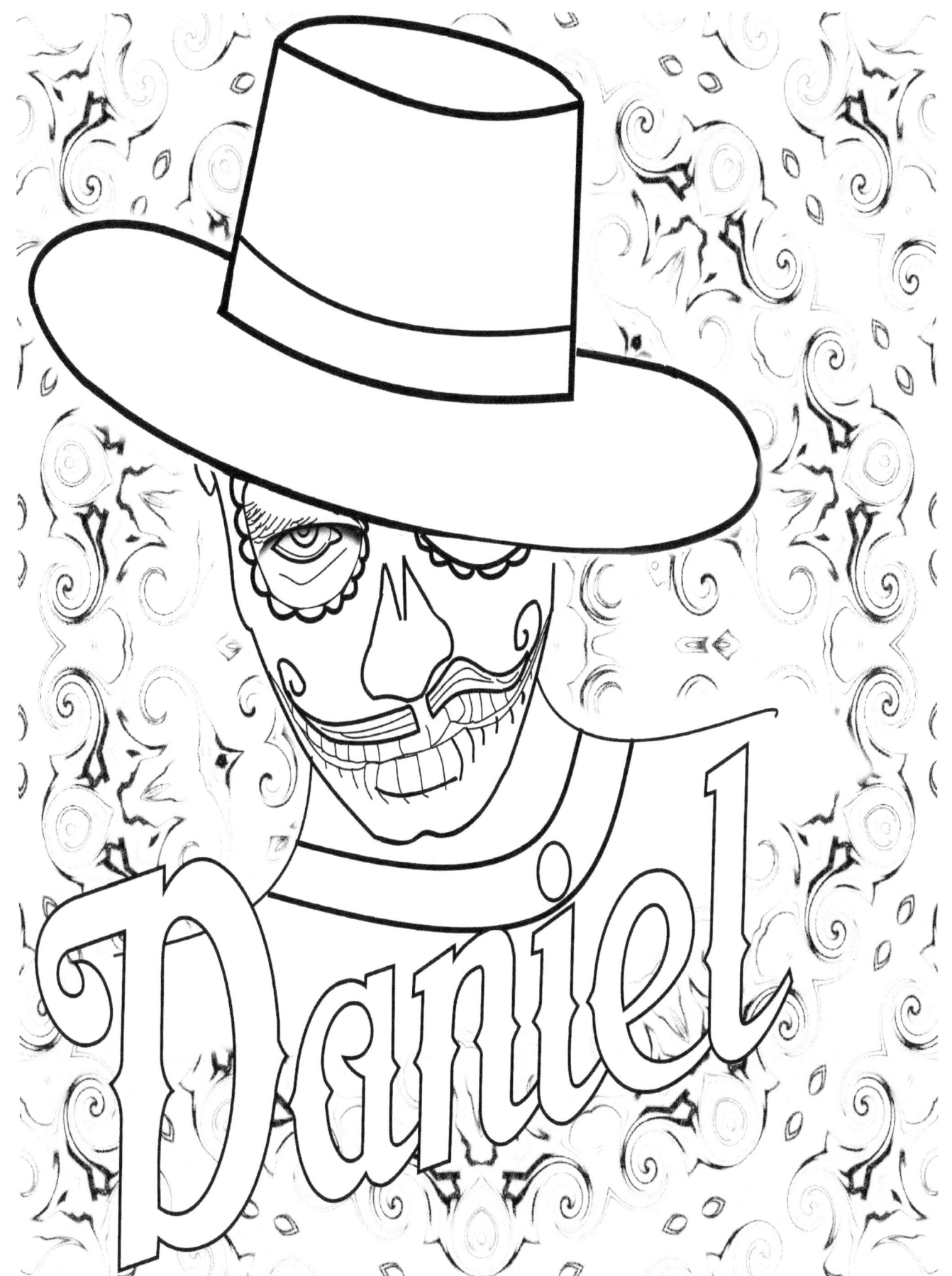

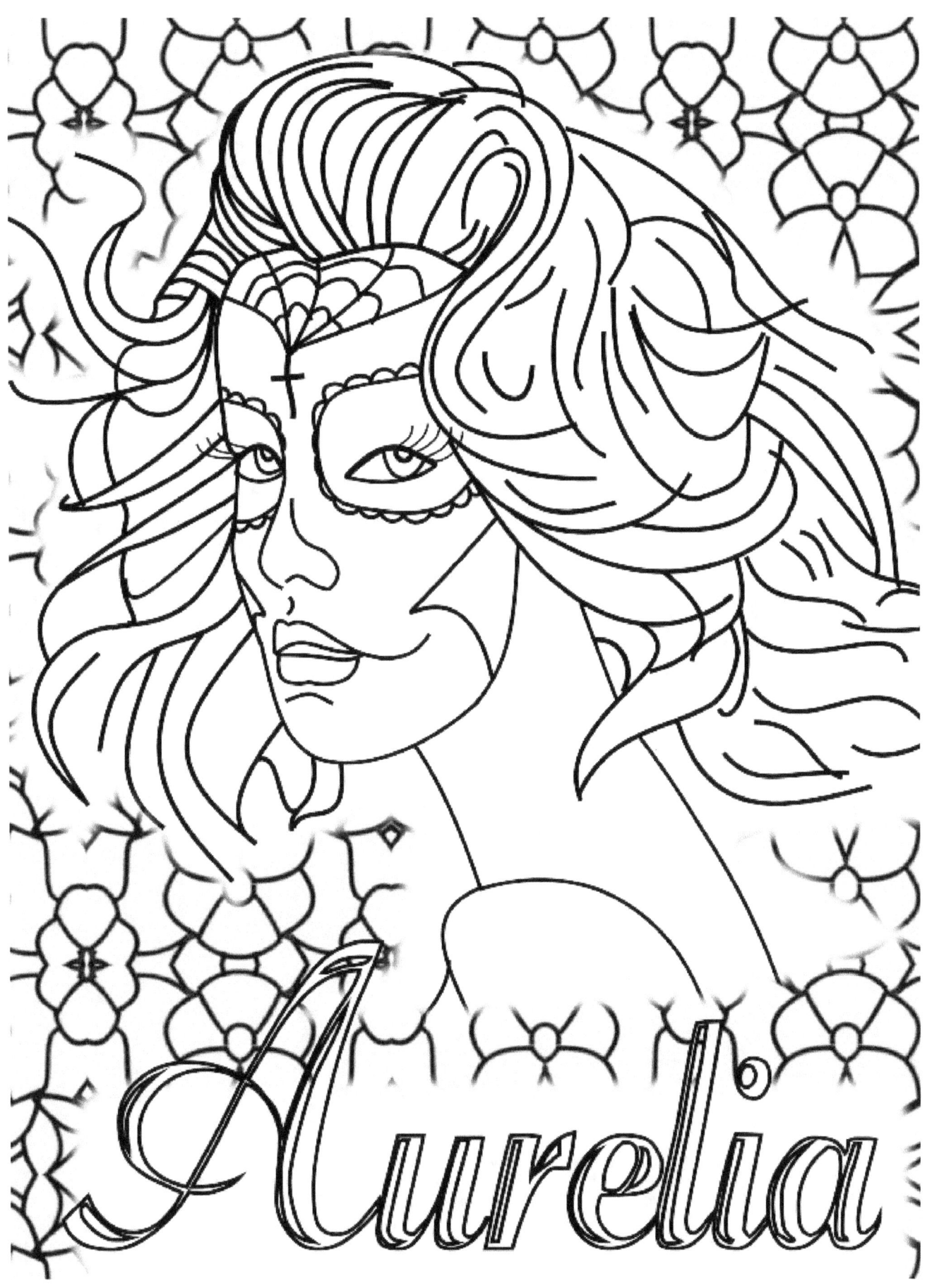

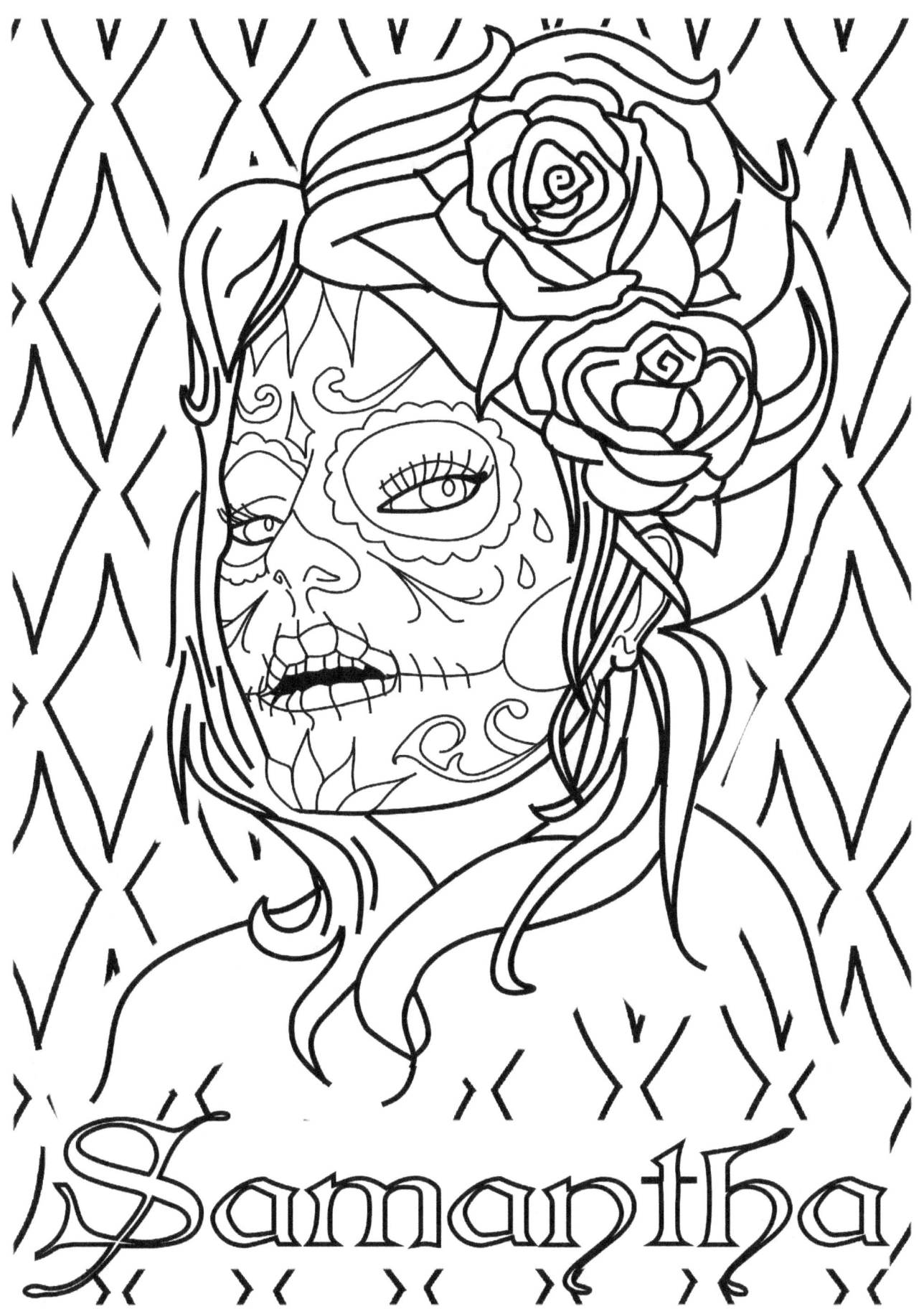

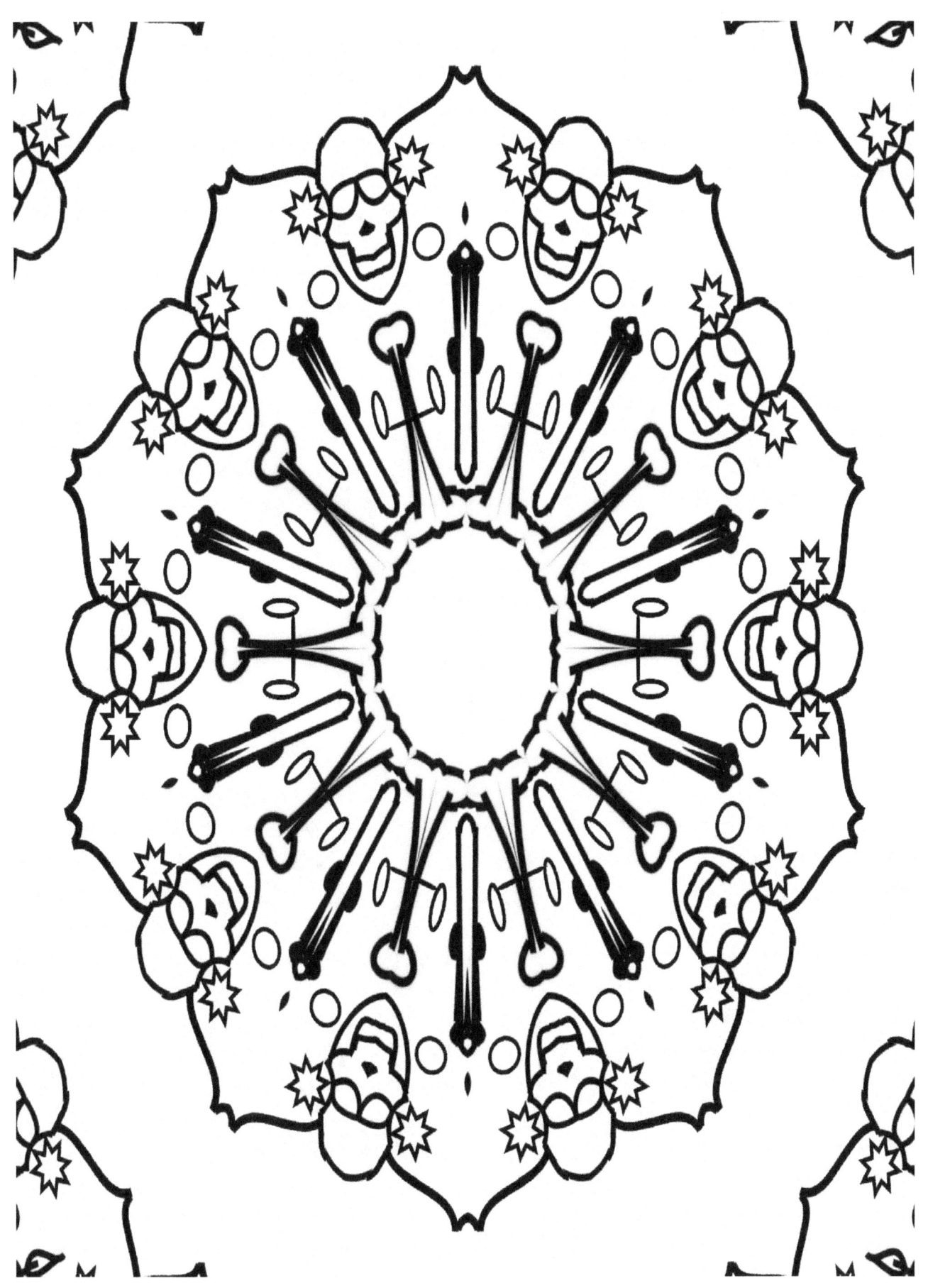

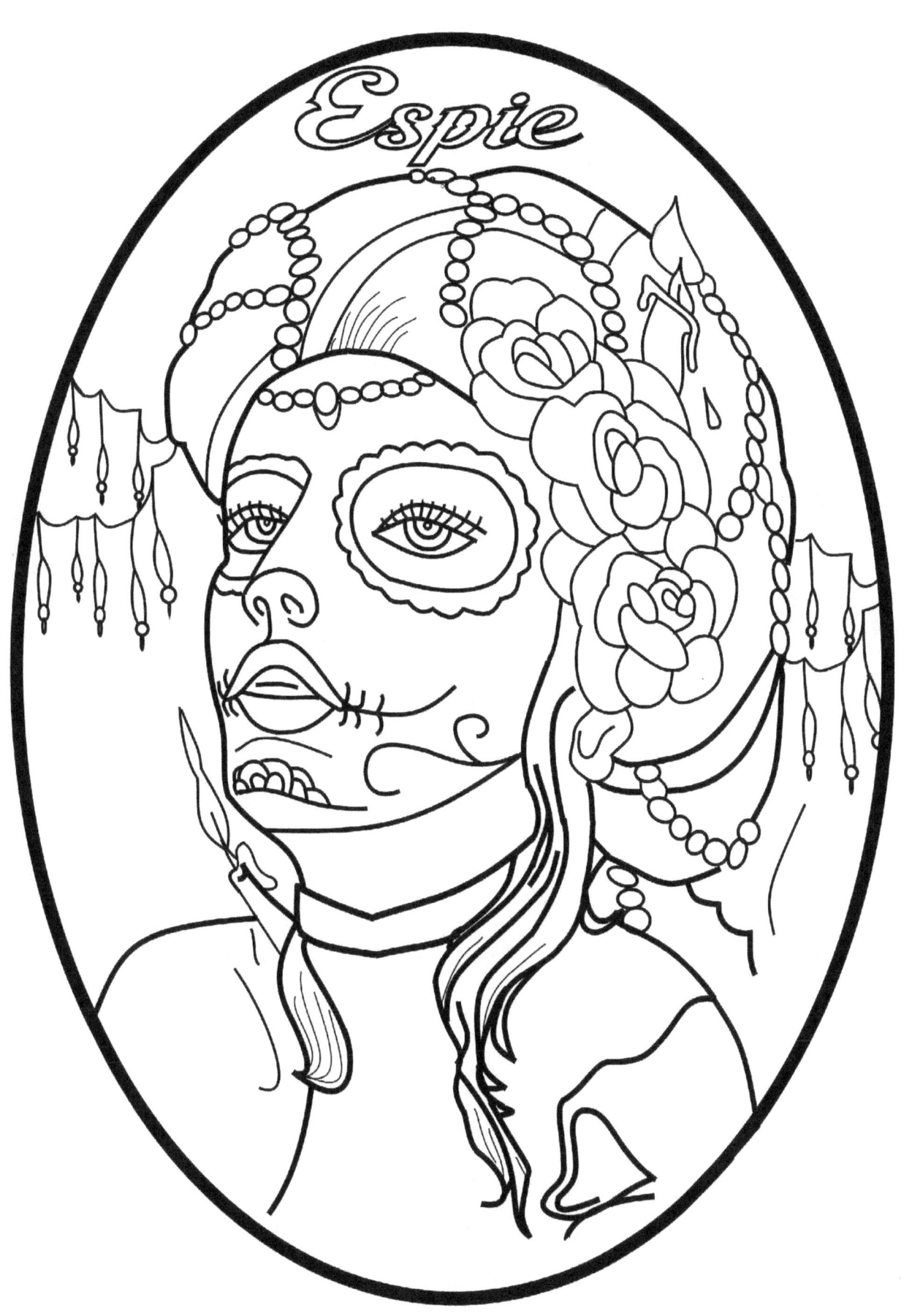

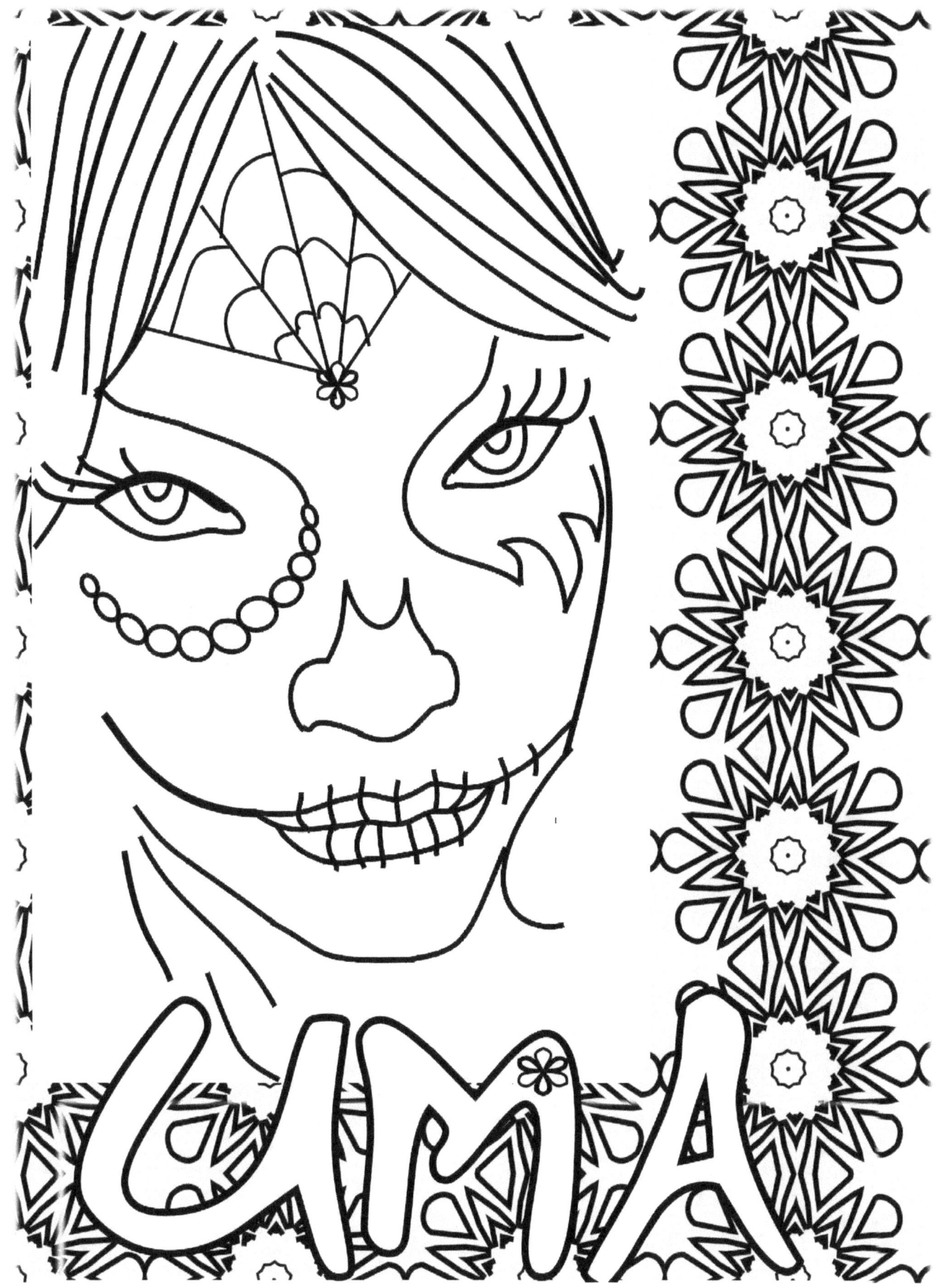

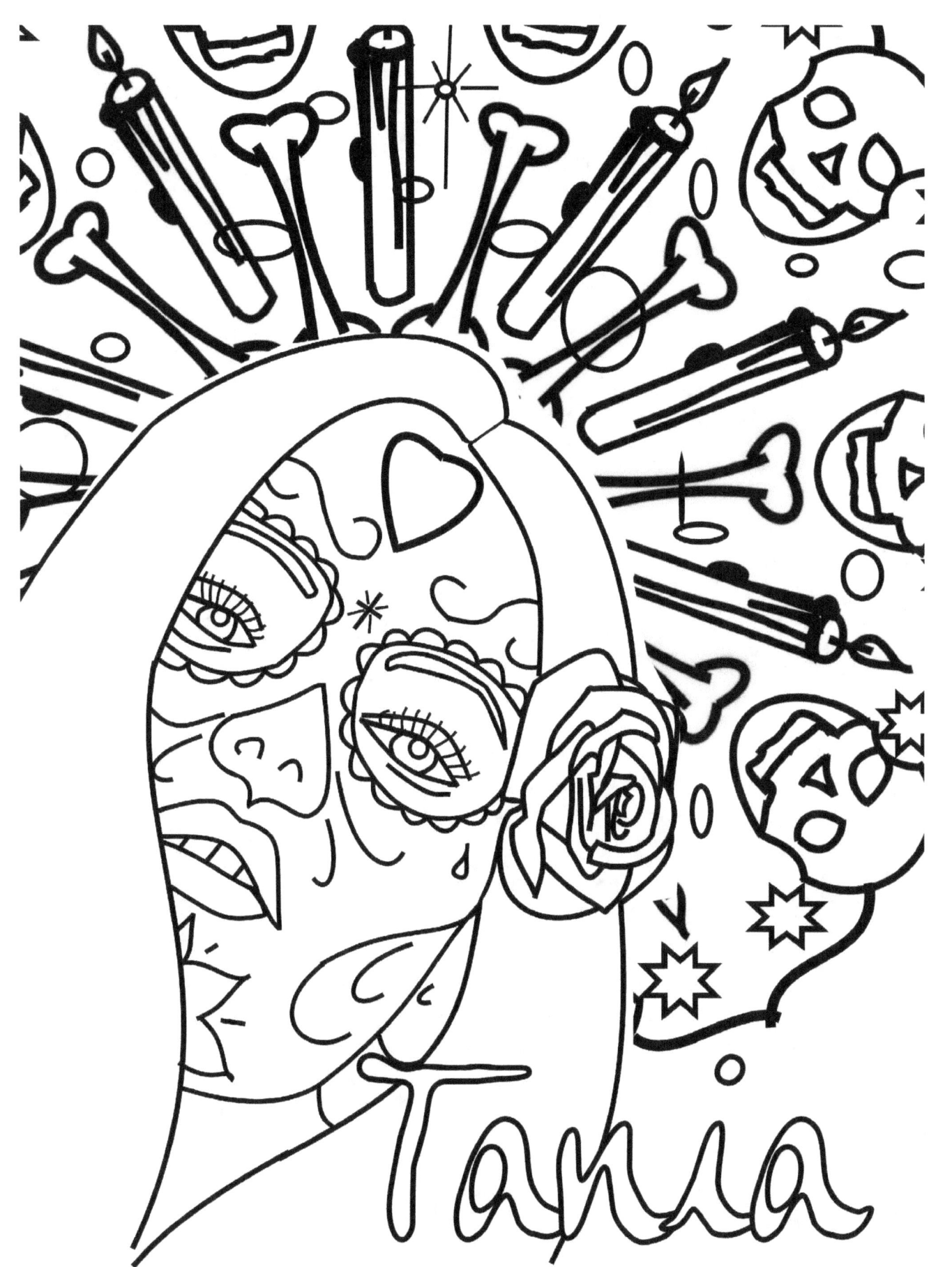

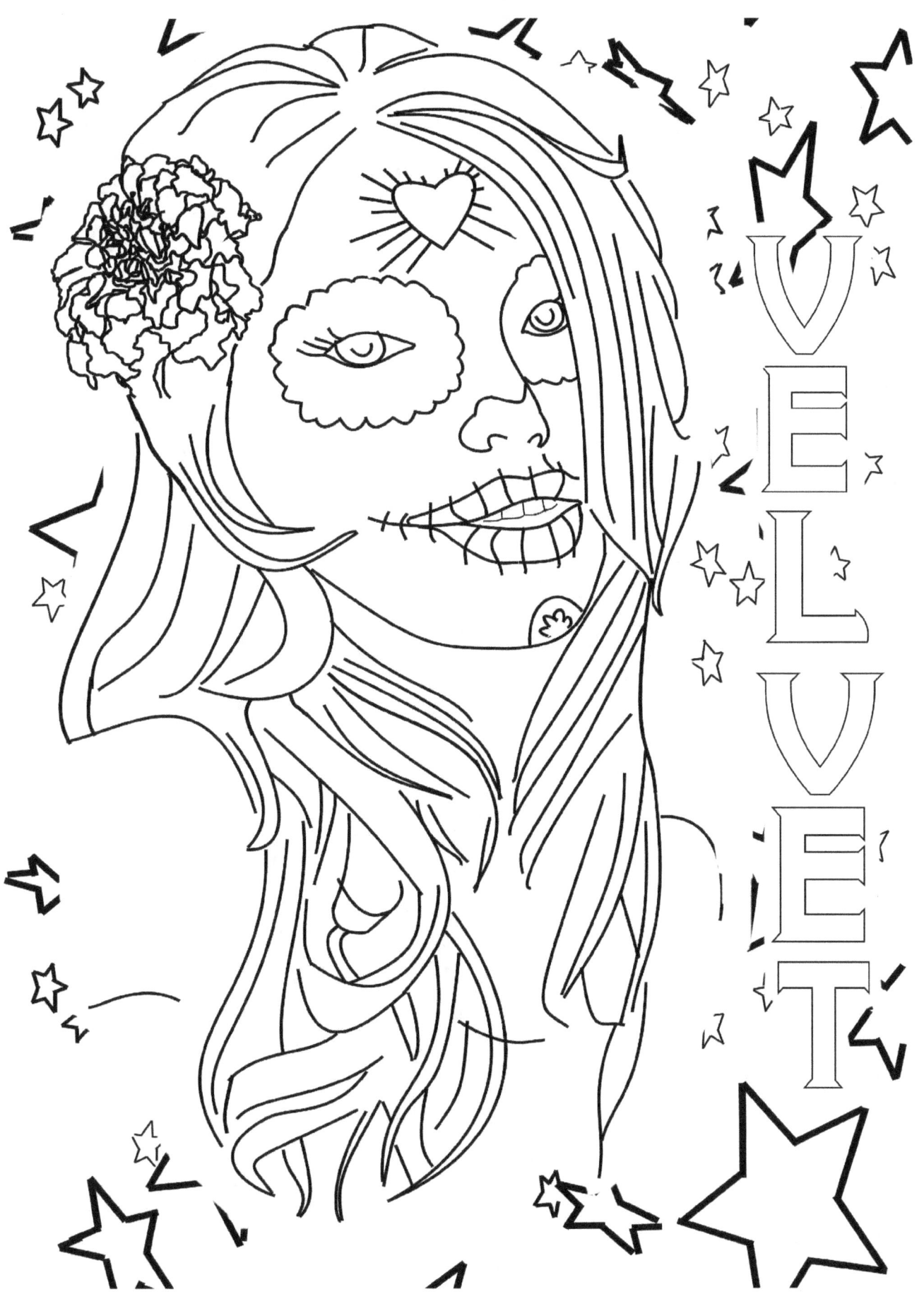

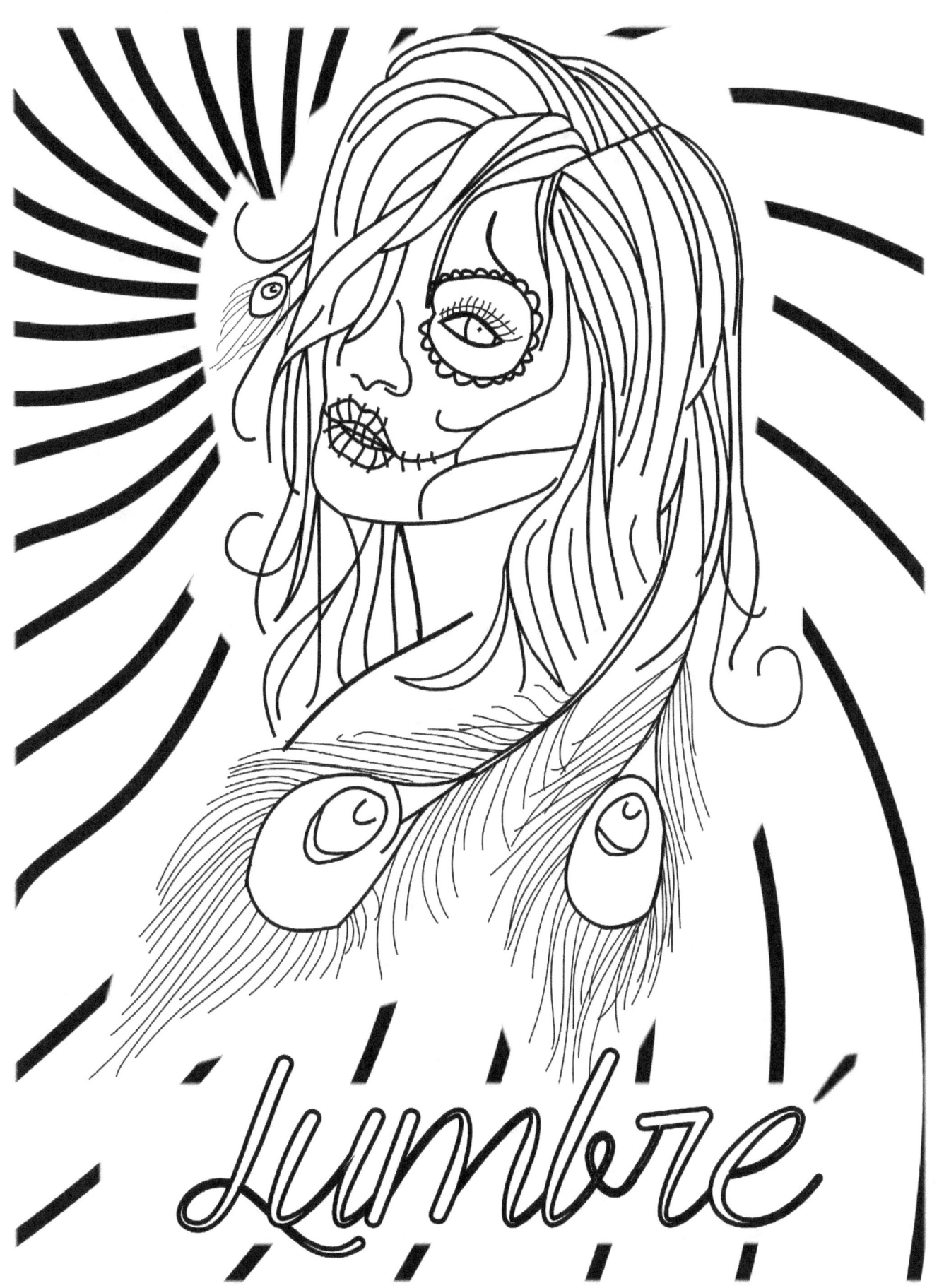

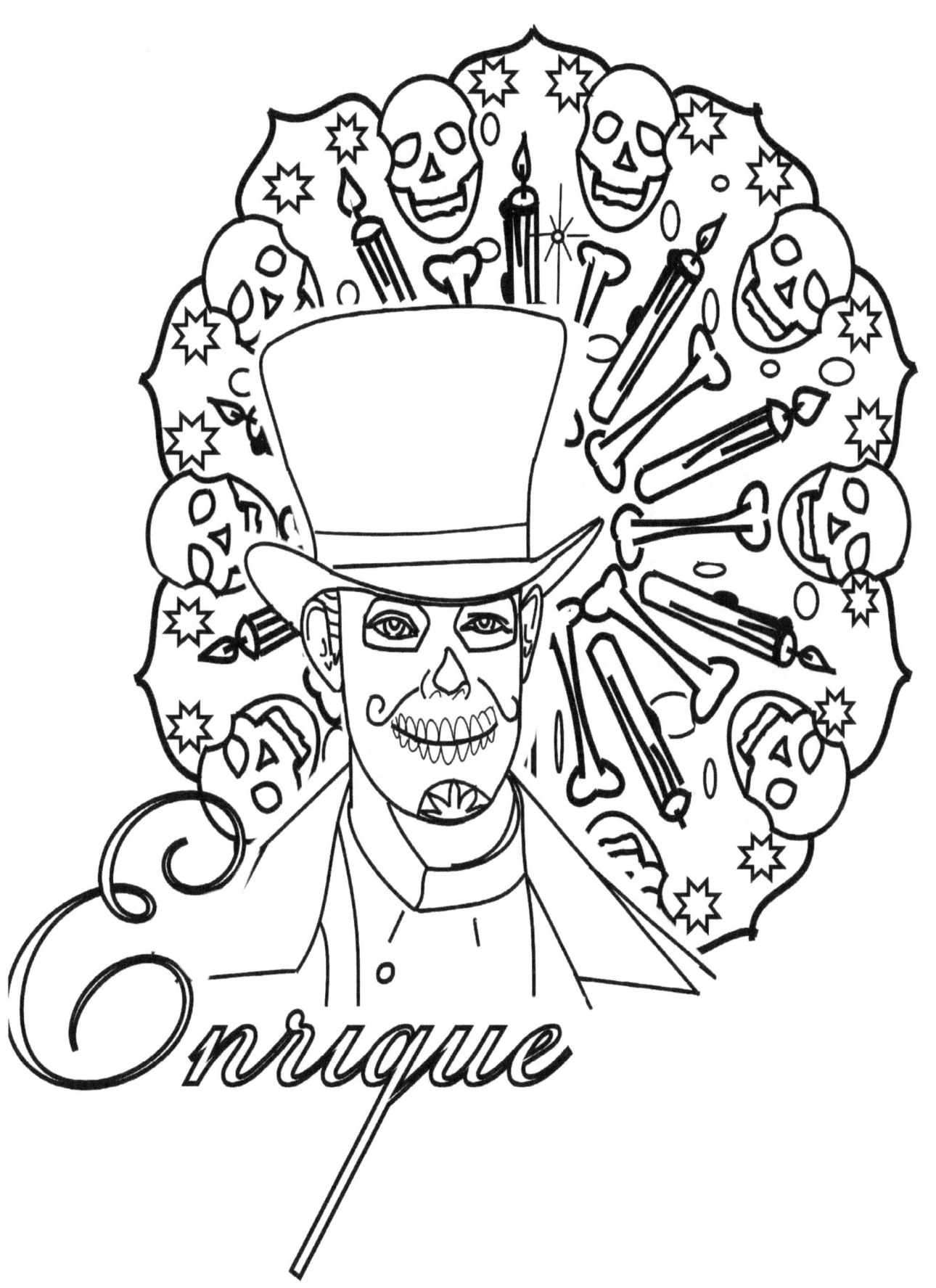

ESPERANZA

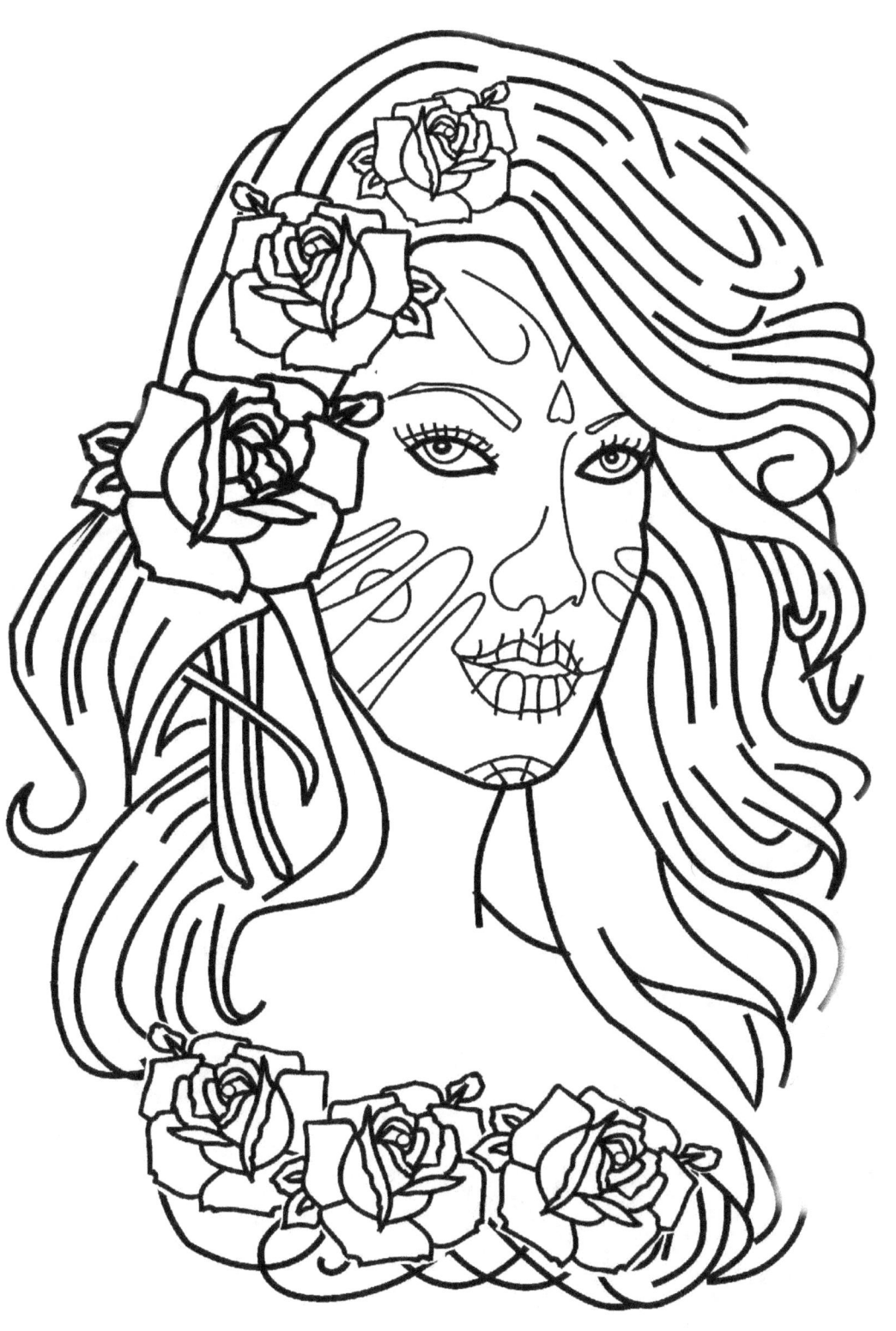

Papel Picado

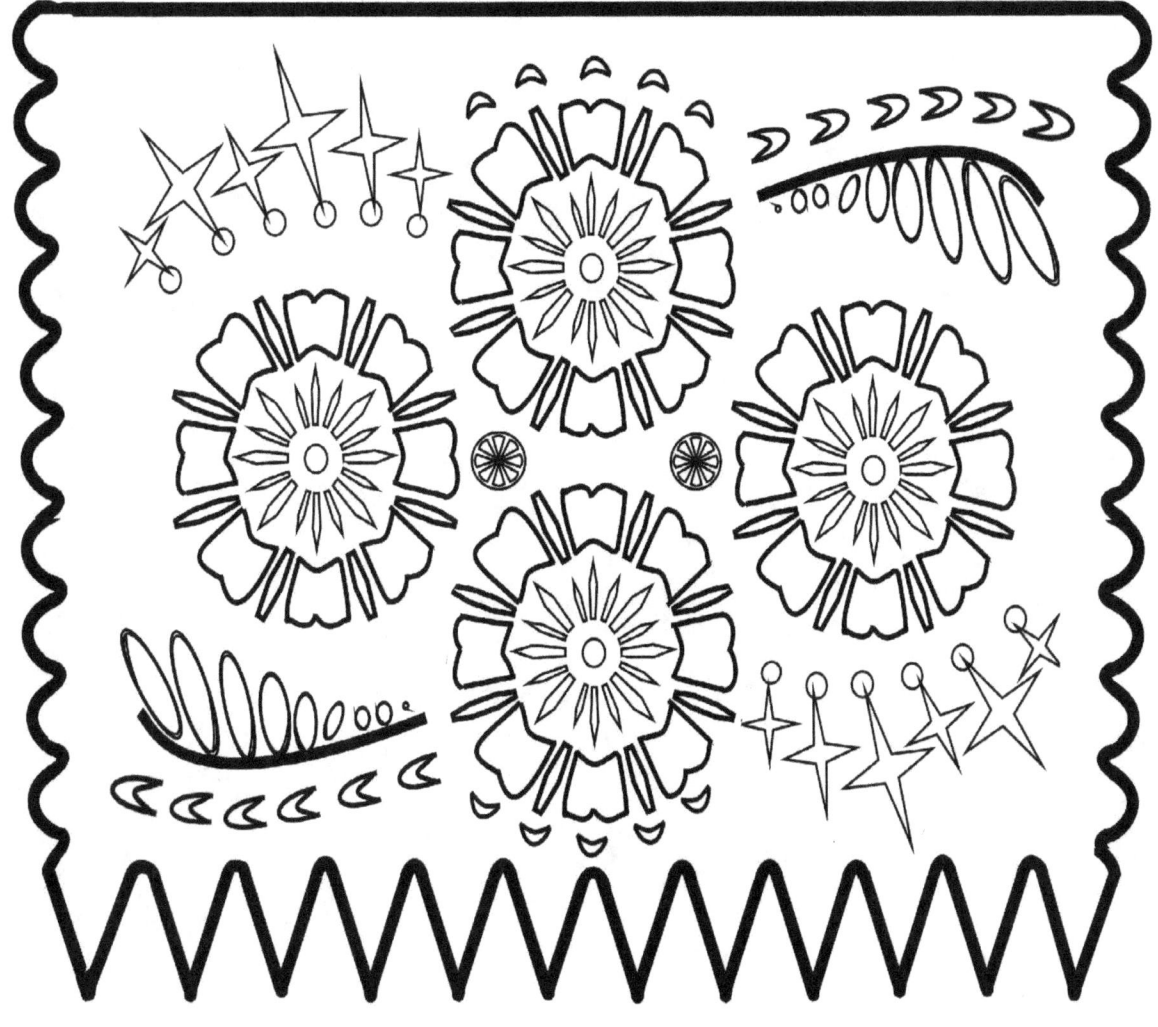

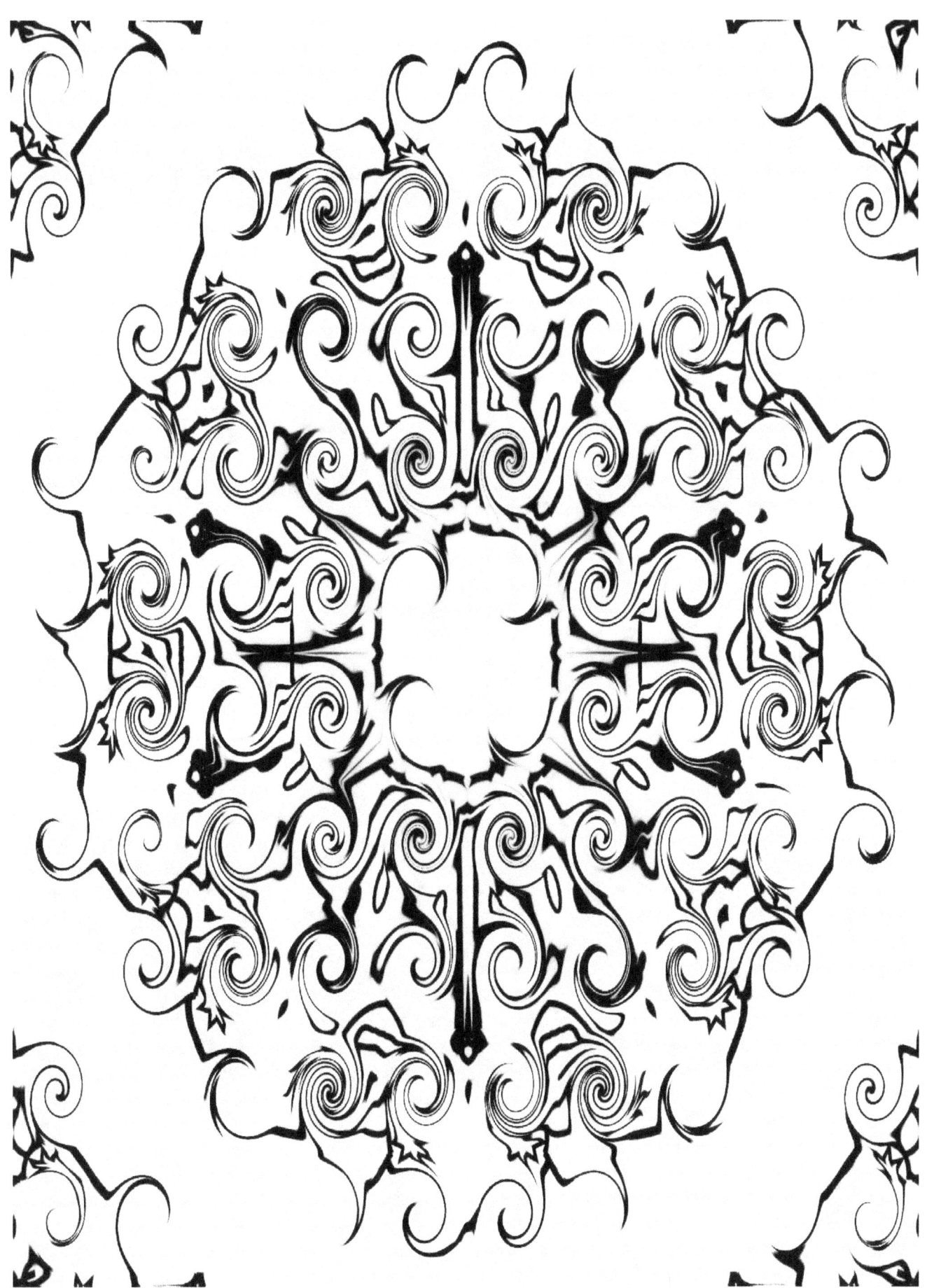

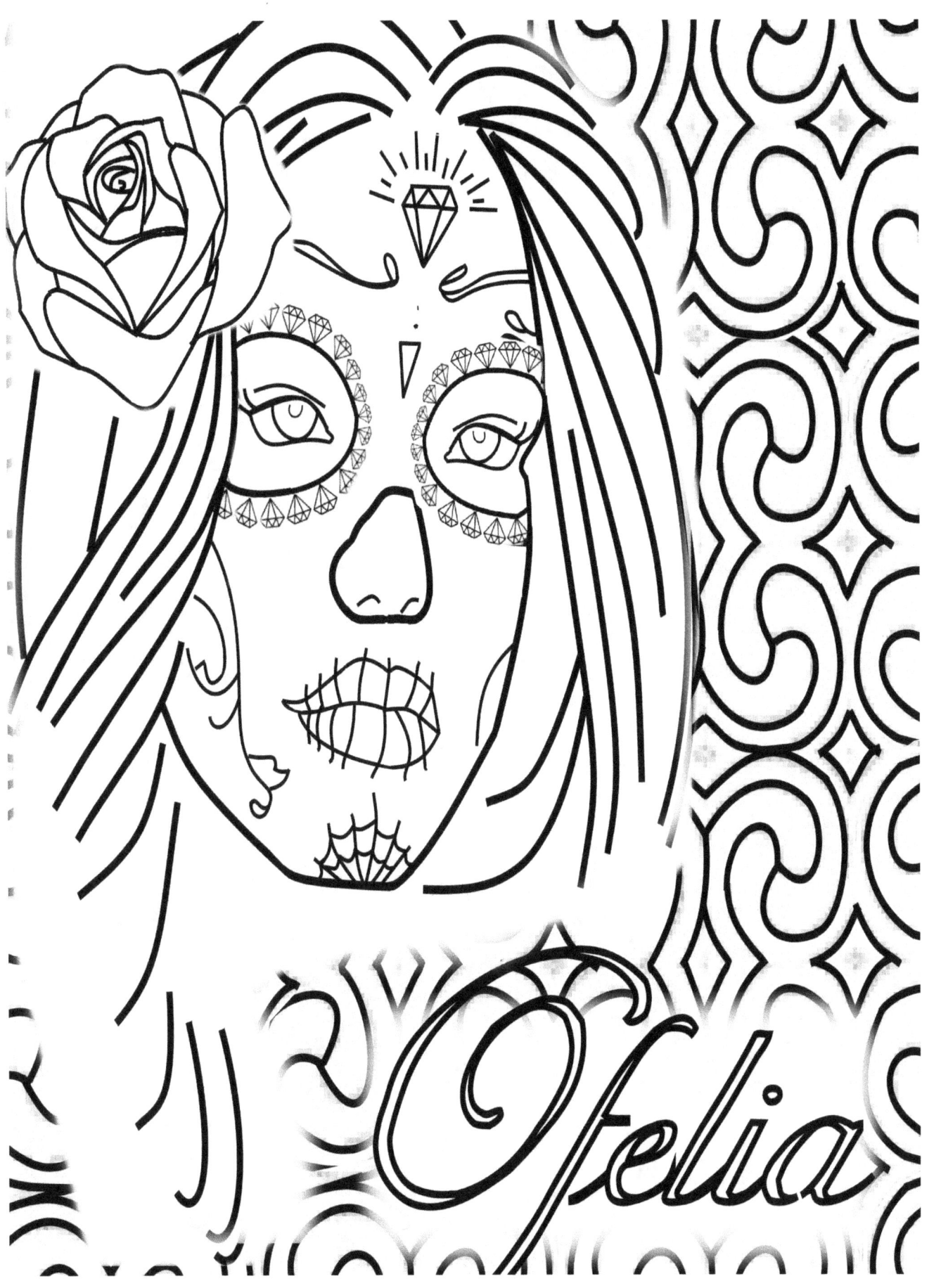

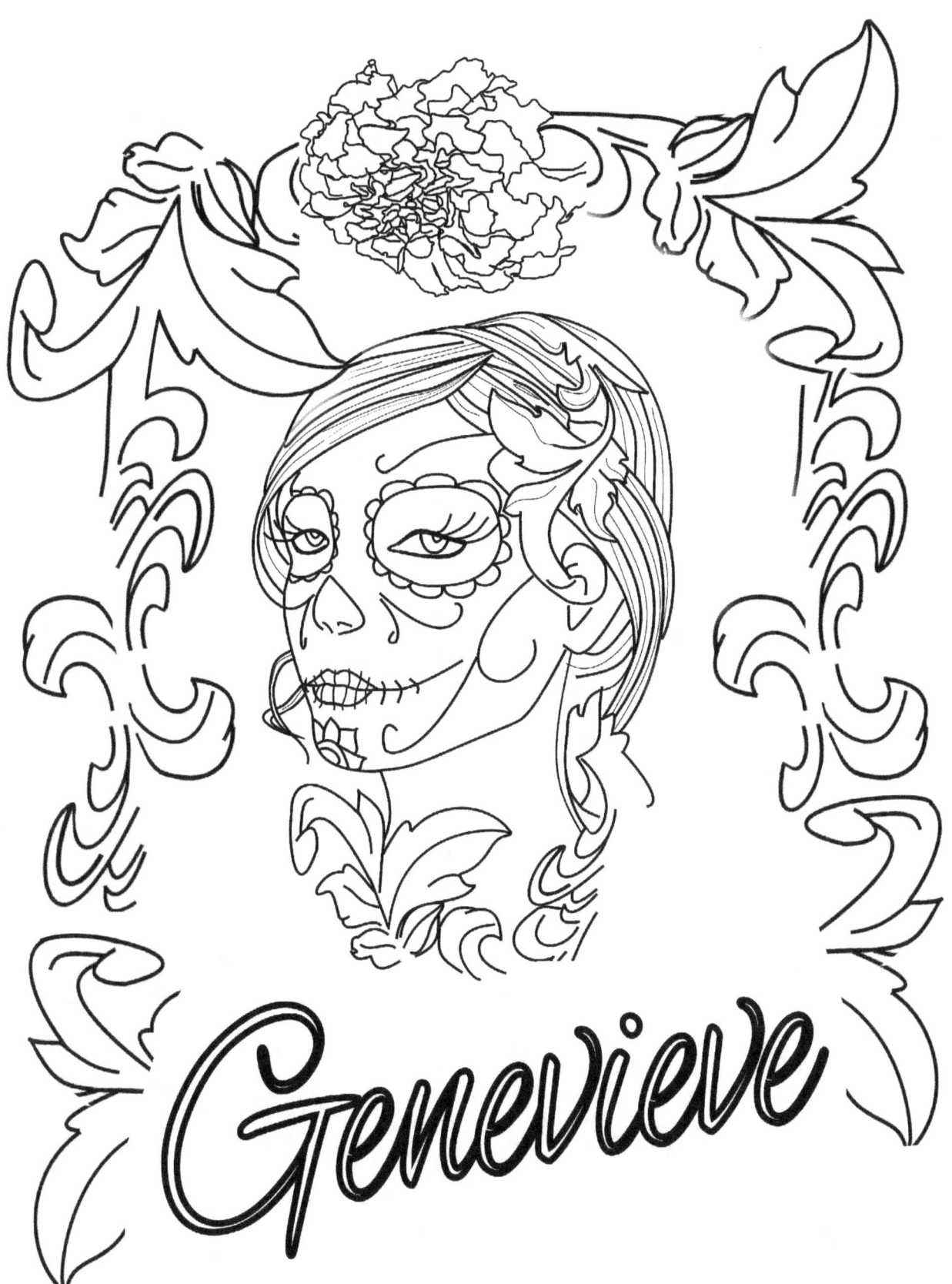

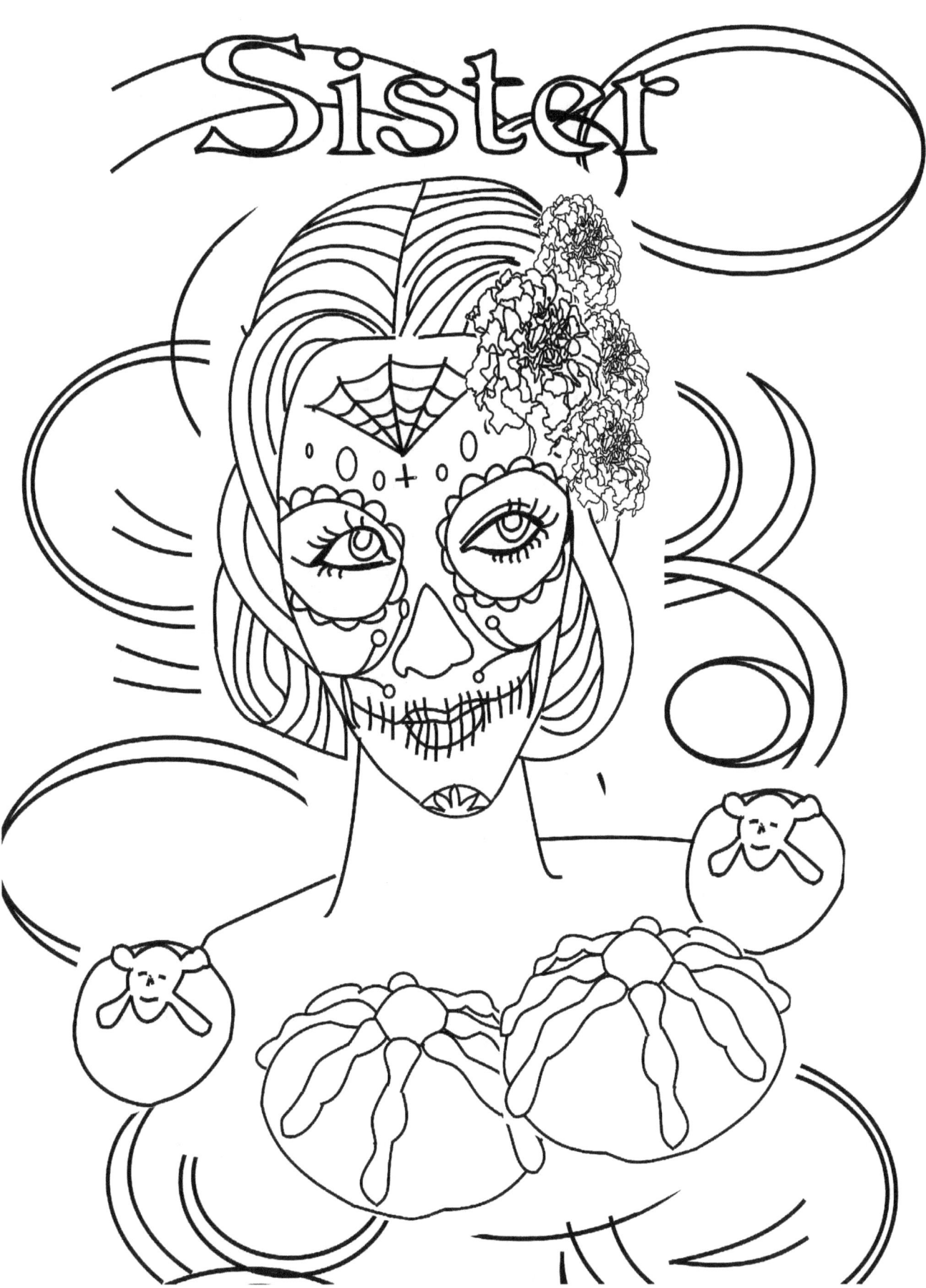

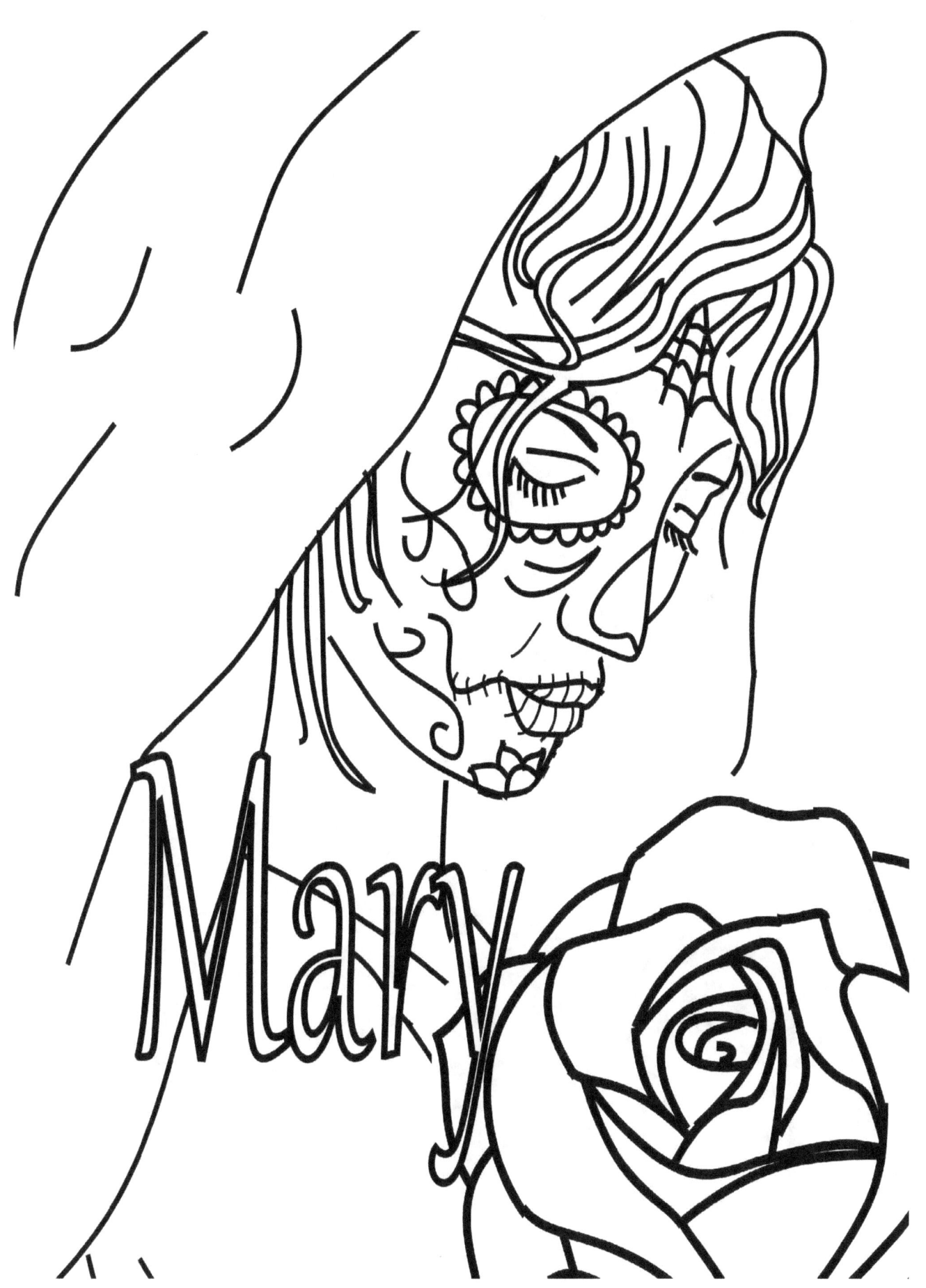

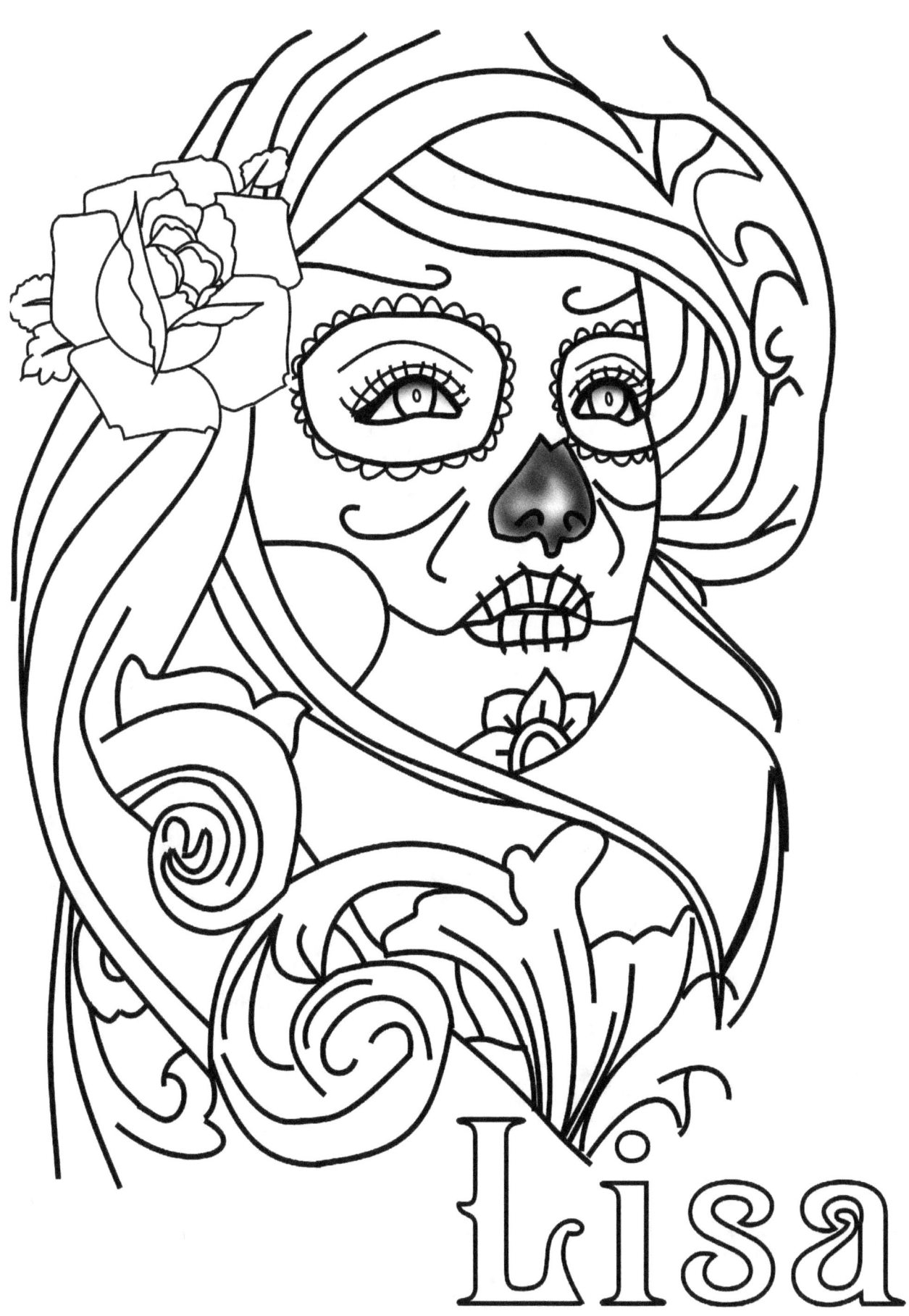

Lisa

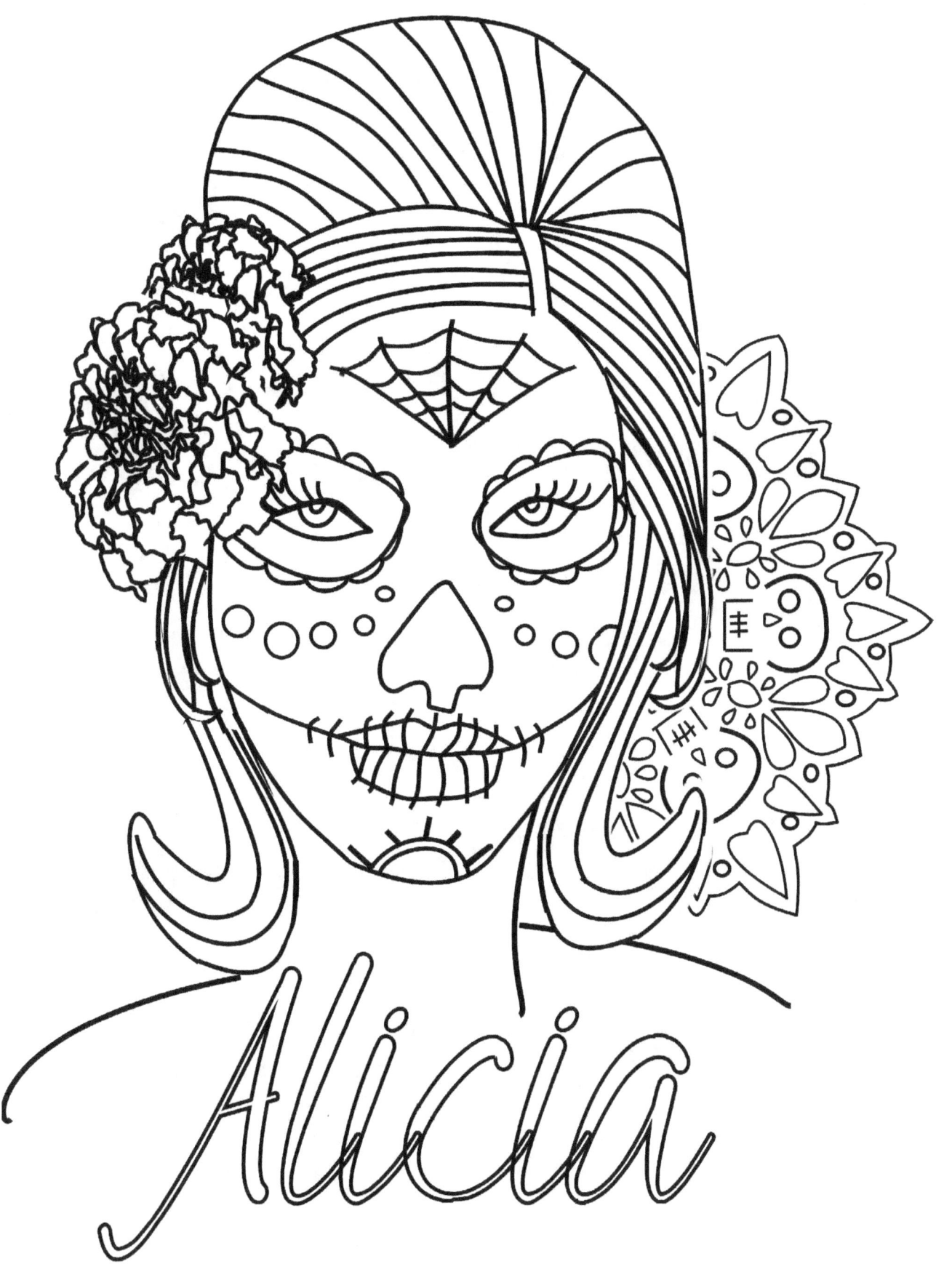

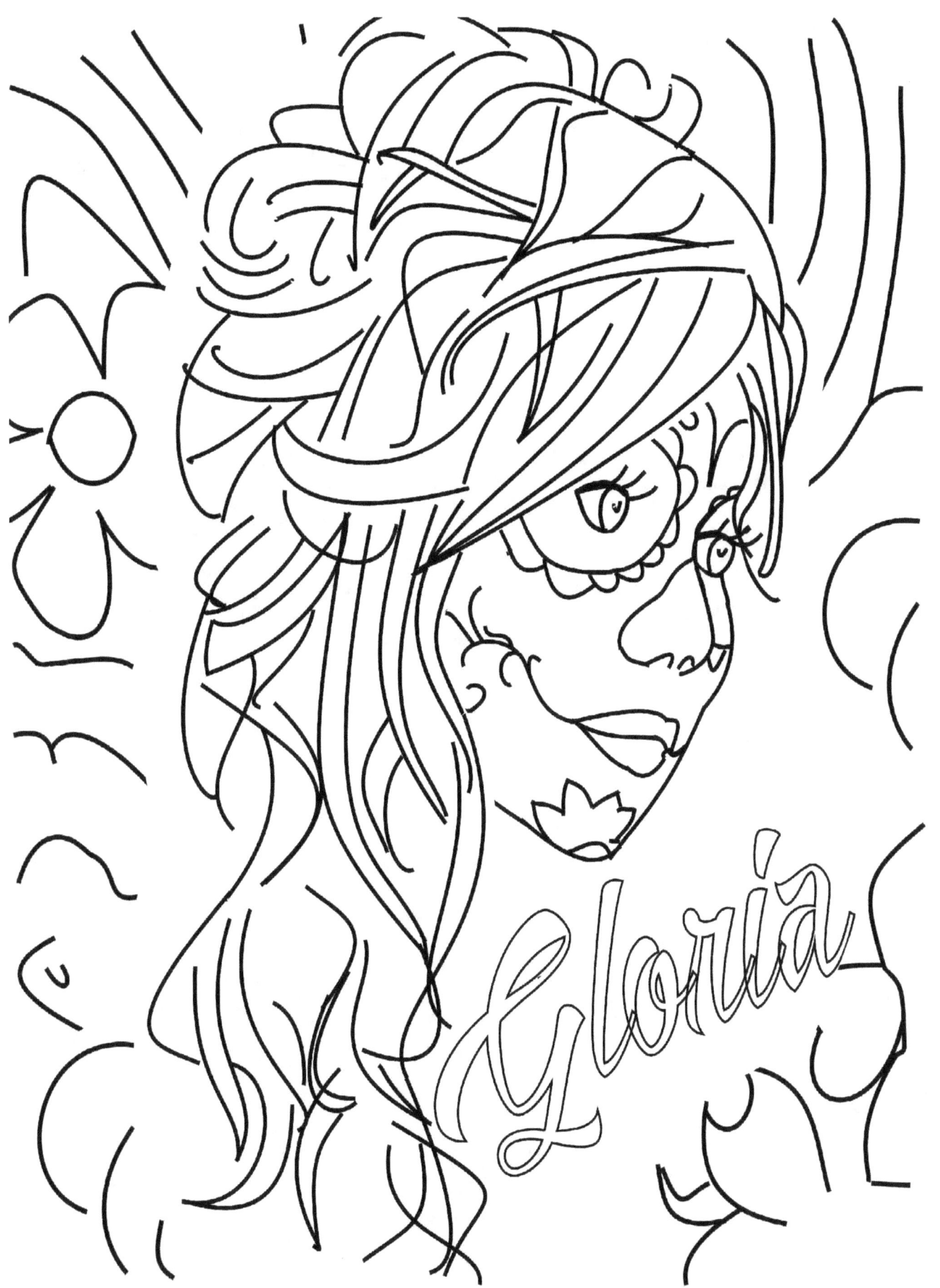

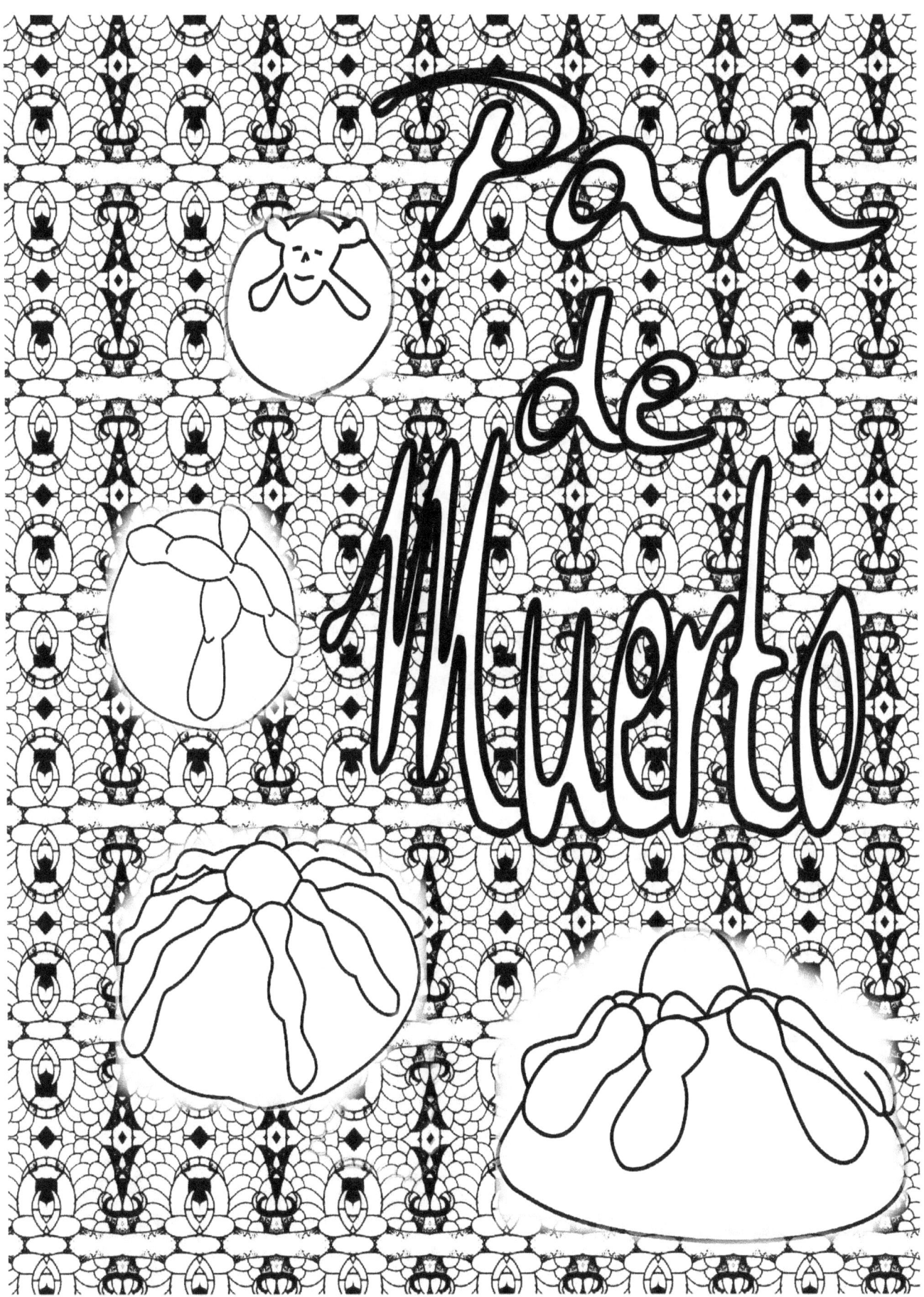

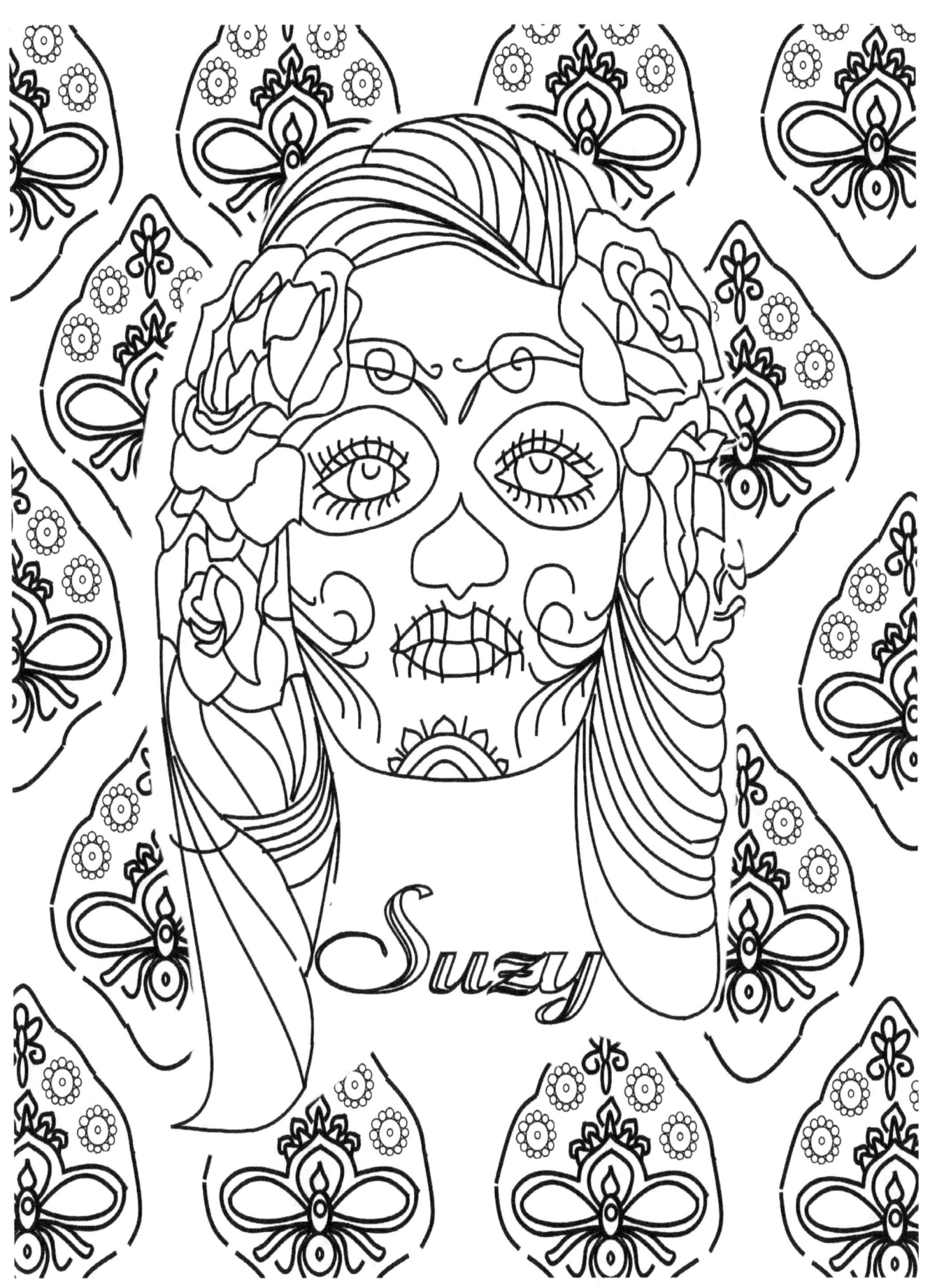

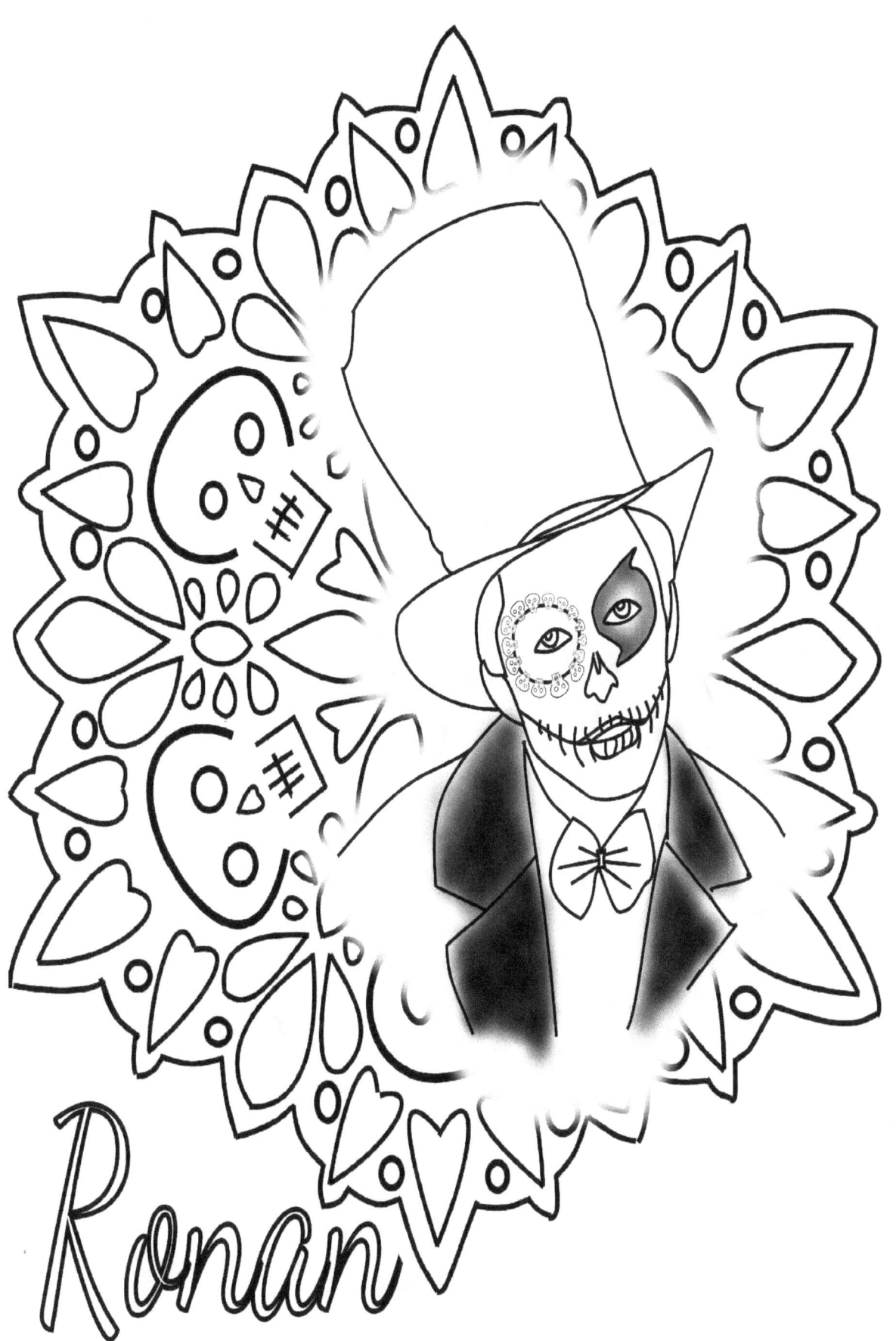

Ronan

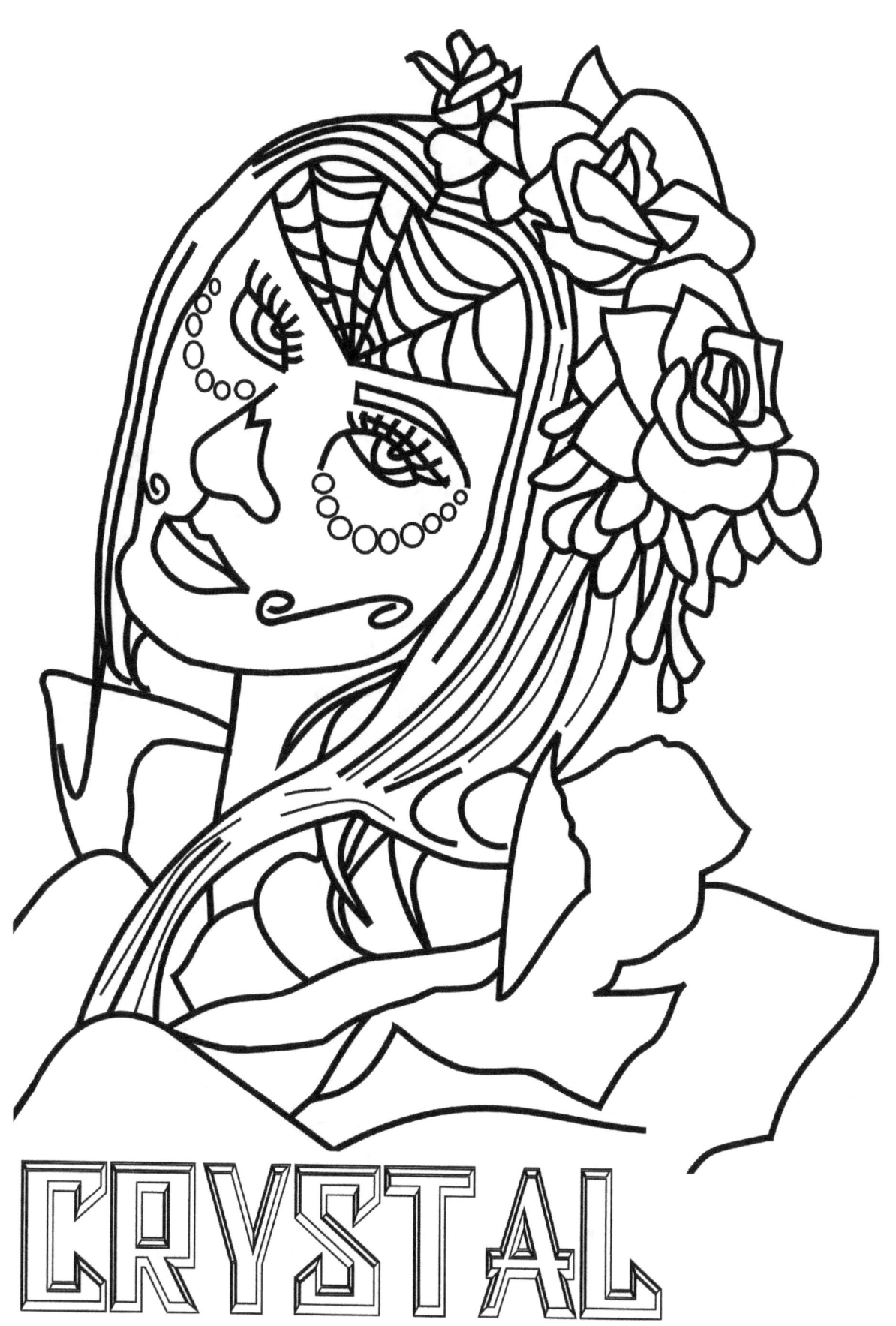

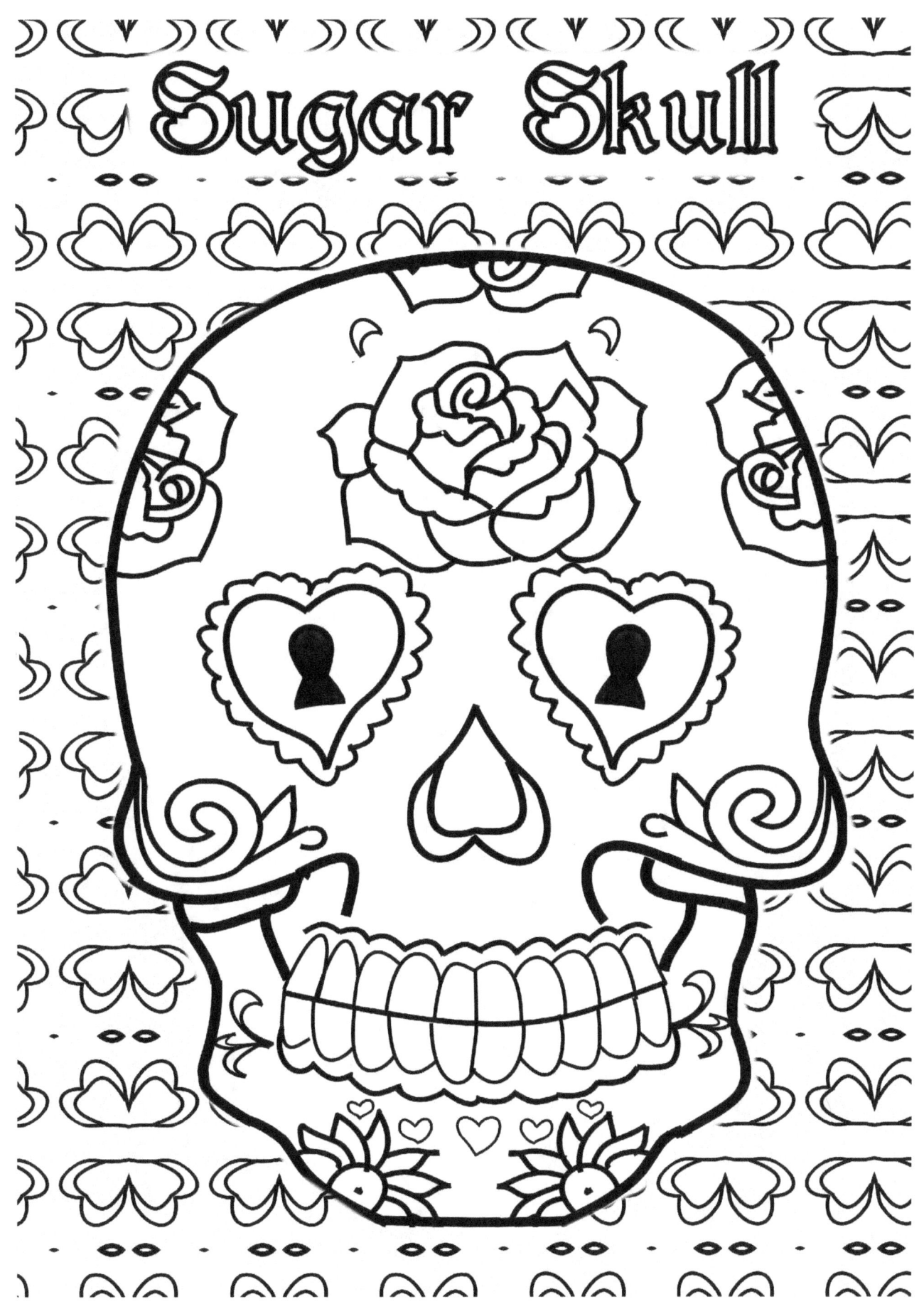

Sugar Skull

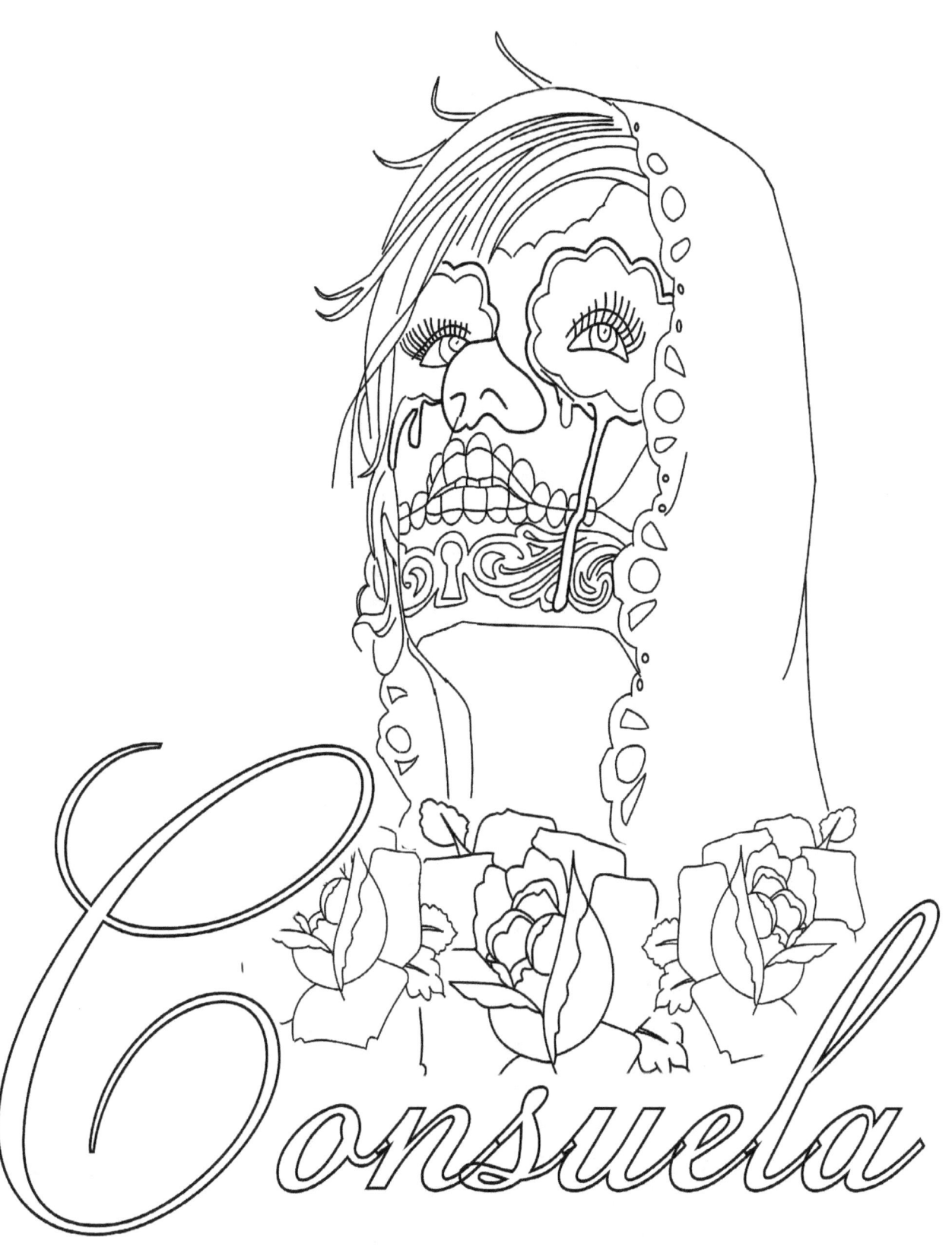

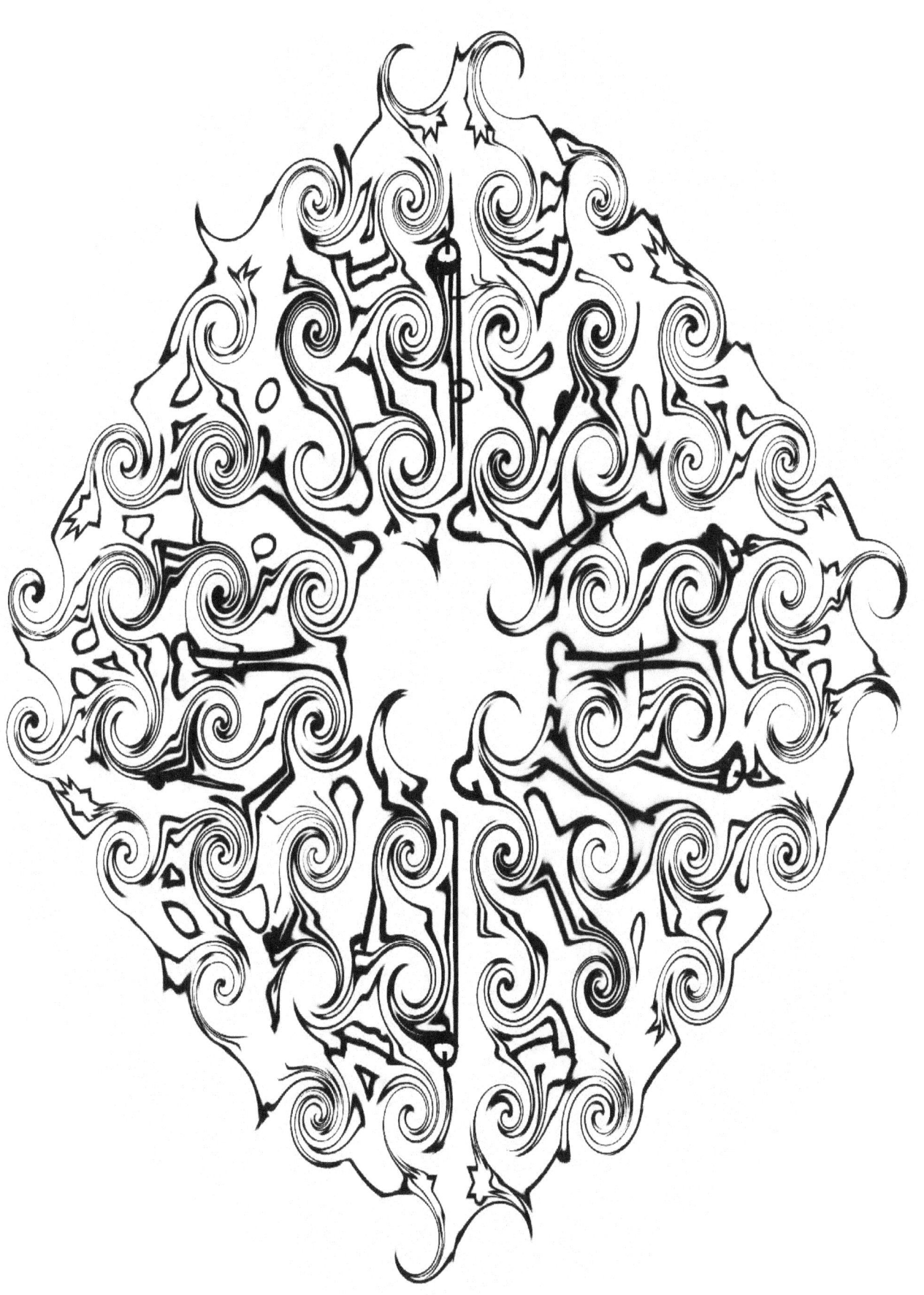

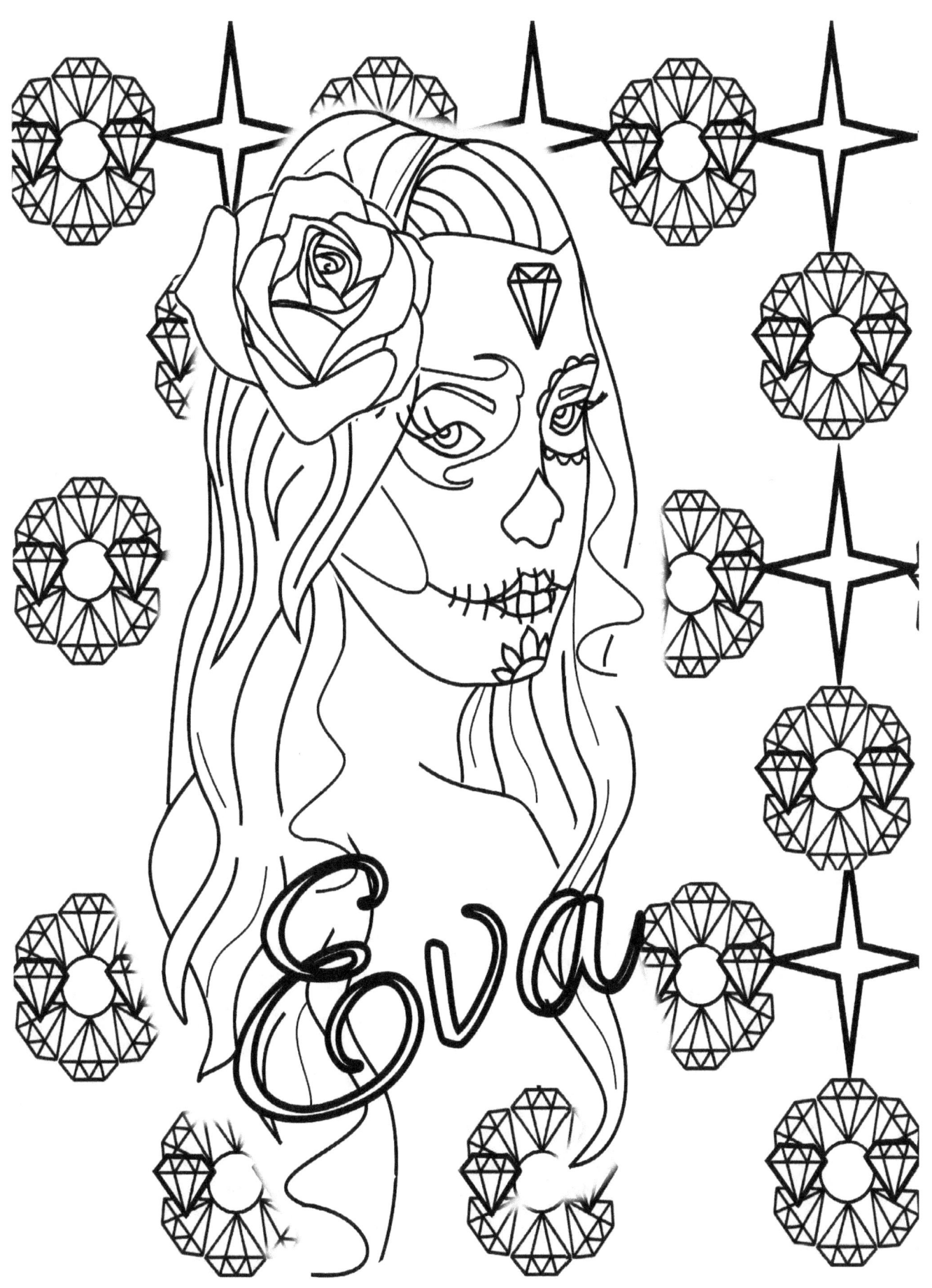

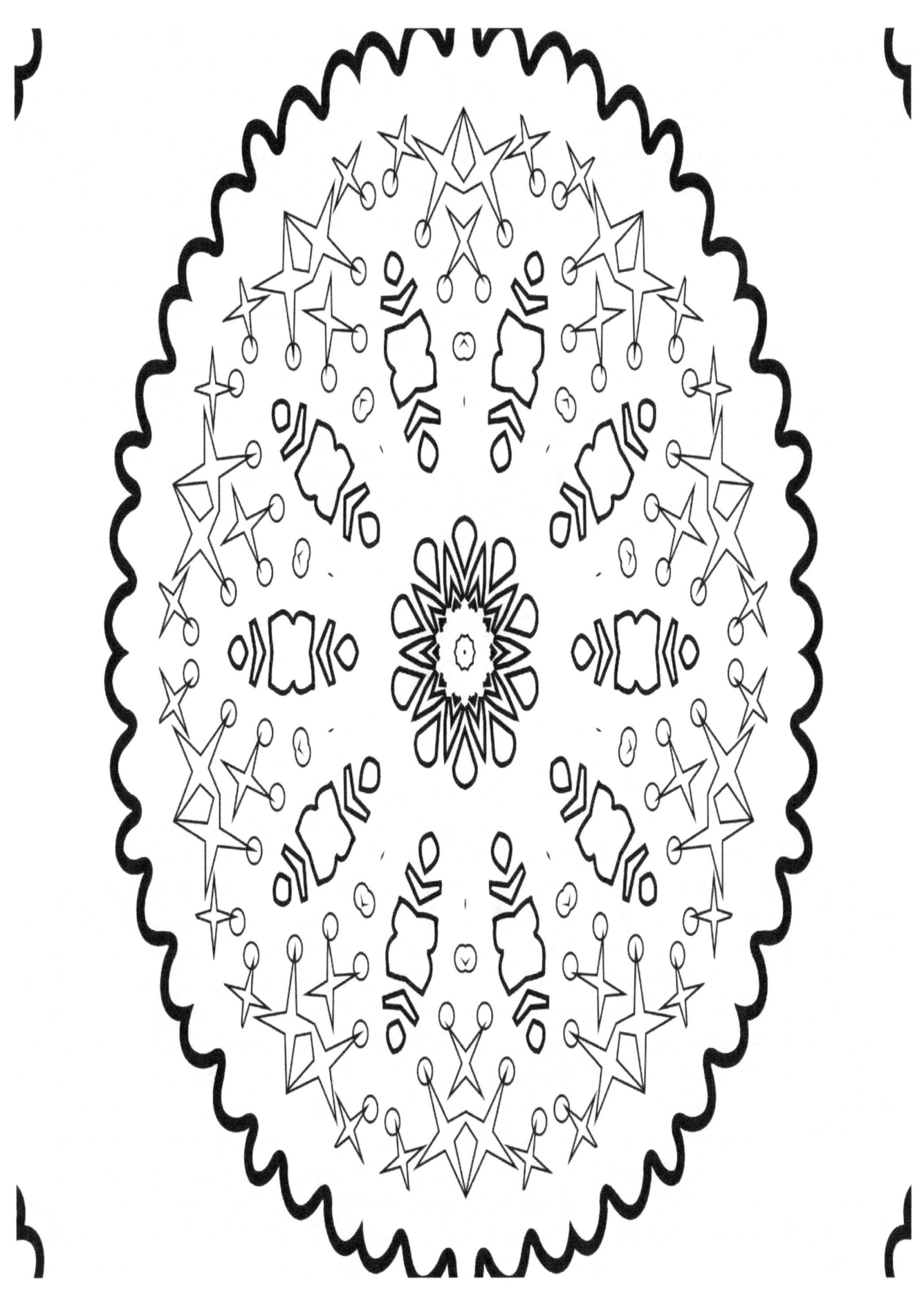

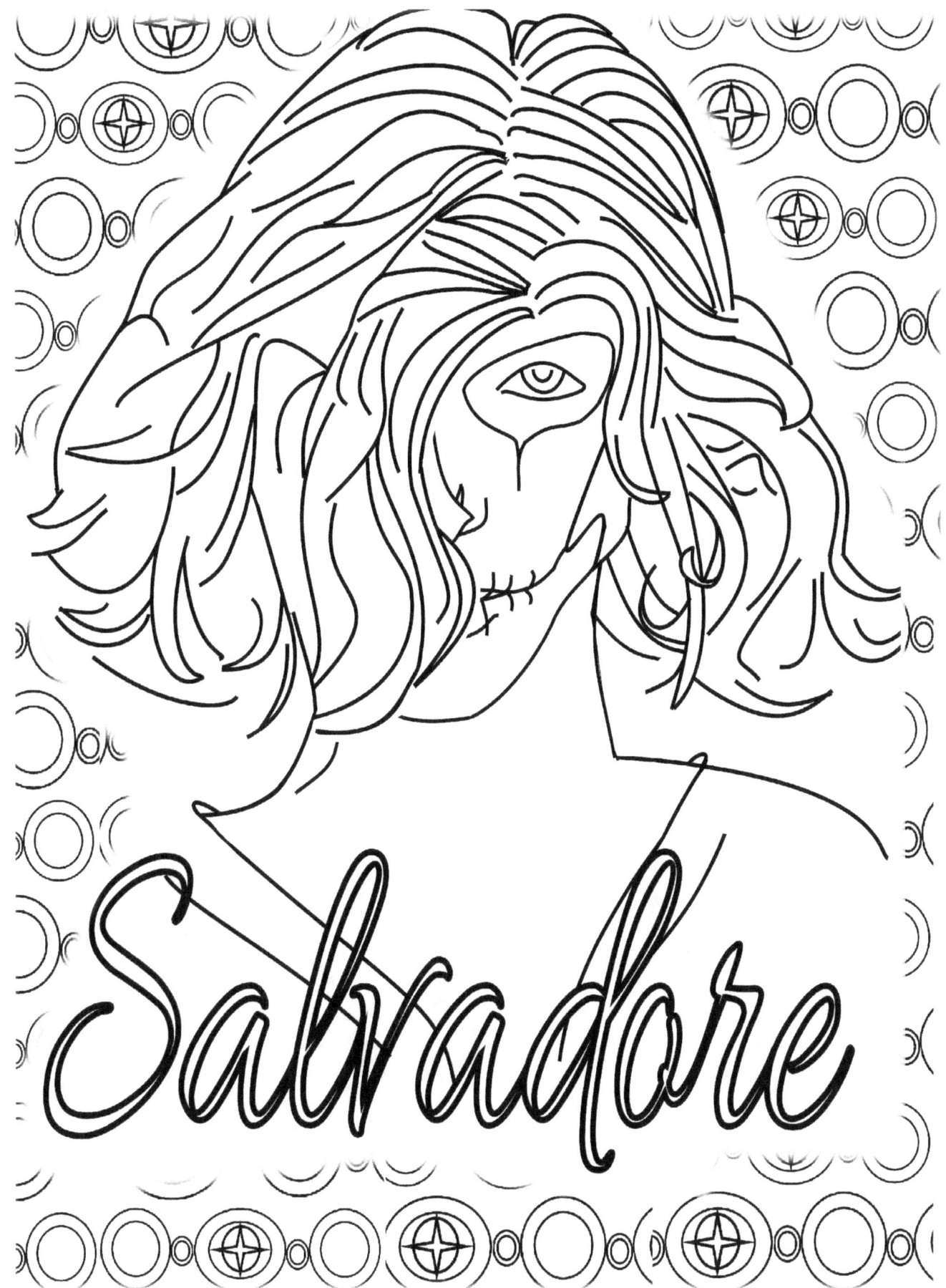

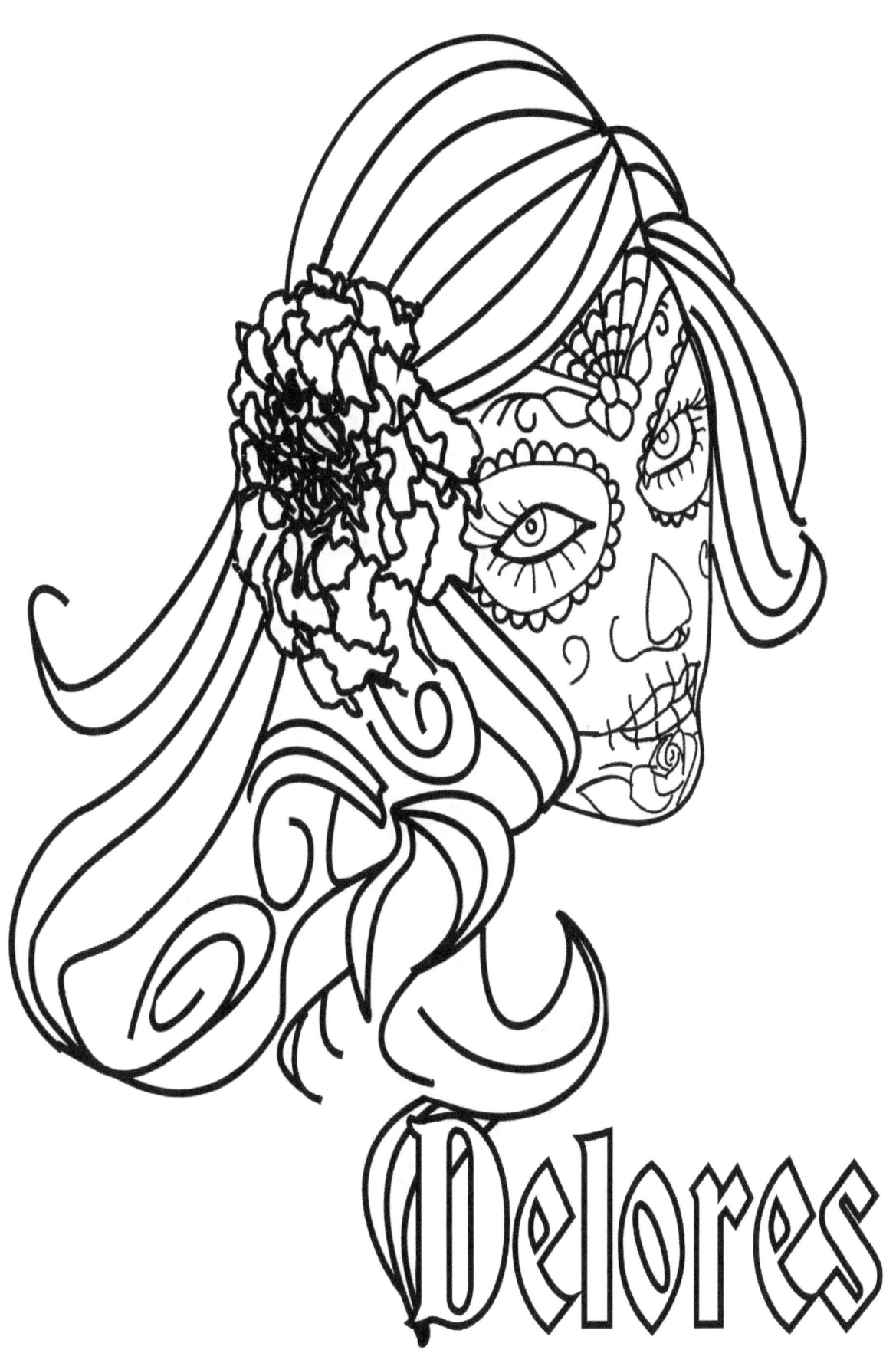

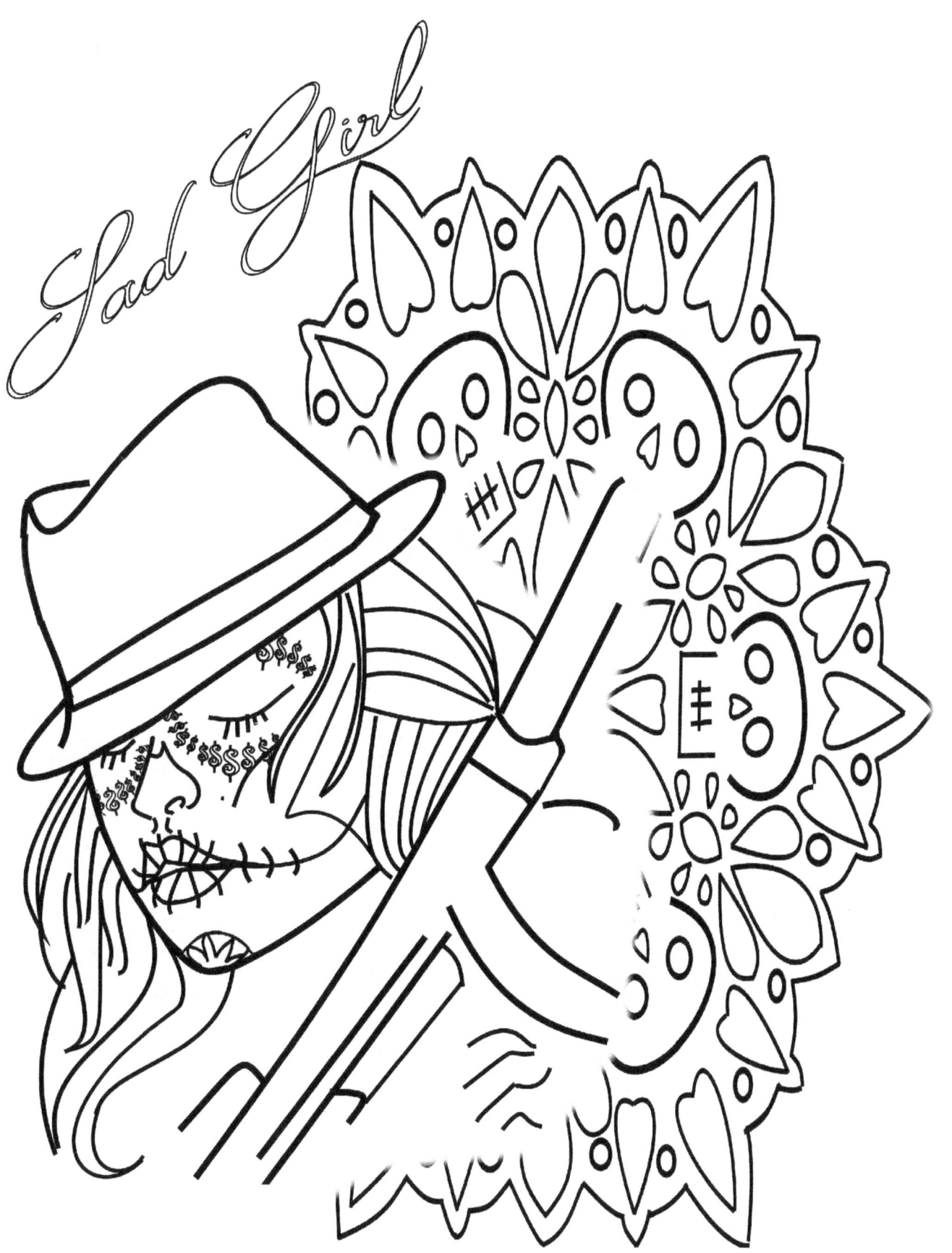

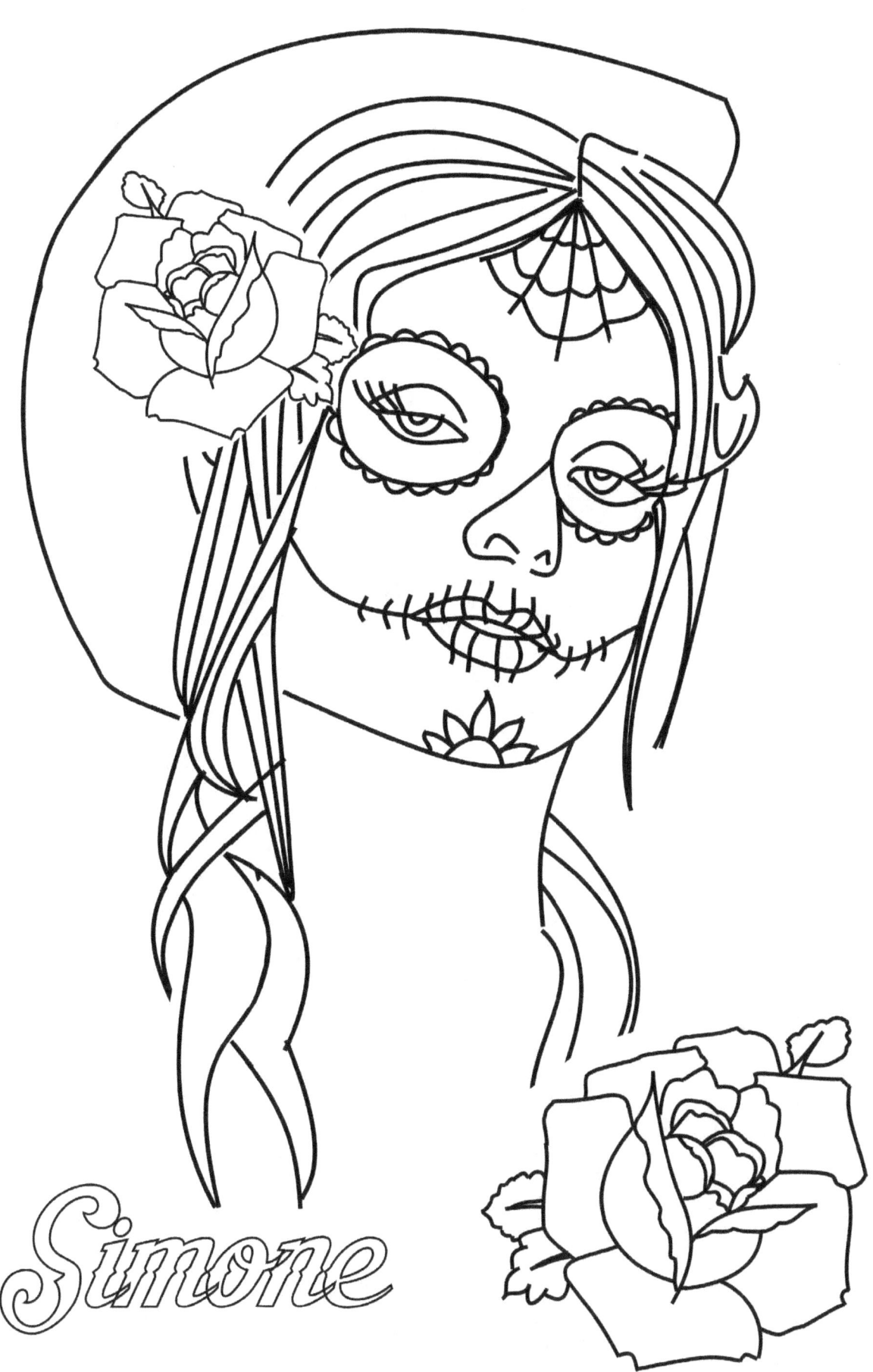

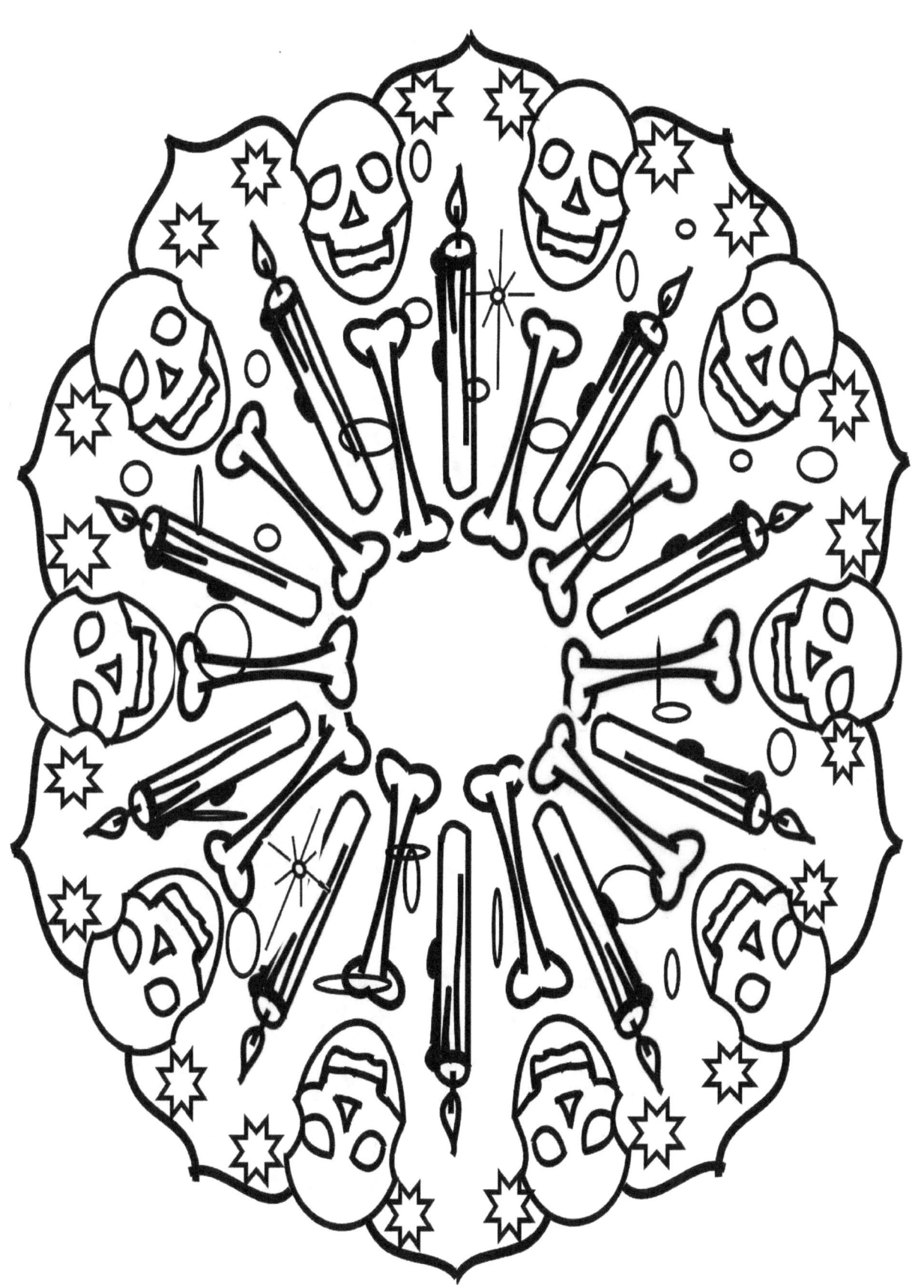

www.ingramcontent.com/pod-product-compliance
Lightning Source LLC
Chambersburg PA
CBHW081553170526
45166CB00009B/2683